T0235257

Communications
in Computer and Information Science   **702**

Commenced Publication in 2007
Founding and Former Series Editors:
Alfredo Cuzzocrea, Orhun Kara, Dominik Ślęzak, and Xiaokang Yang

More information about this series at http://www.springer.com/series/7899

Kalinka Branco · Alex Pinto
Daniel Pigatto (Eds.)

Communication in Critical Embedded Systems

First Workshop, WoCCES 2013
Brasília, Brazil, May 10, 2013
Second Workshop, WoCCES 2014
Florianópolis, Brazil, May 9, 2014
Third Workshop, WoCCES 2015
Vitória, Brazil, May 22, 2015
4th Workshop, WoCCES 2016
Salvador, Brazil, June 3, 2016
Revised Selected Papers

 Springer

Editors
Kalinka Branco
Institute of Mathematics and Computer
  Sciences
University of São Paulo
São Carlos, São Paulo
Brazil

Alex Pinto
Department of Control Engineering
  and Automation
Federal University of Santa Catarina
Blumenau, Santa Catarina
Brazil

Daniel Pigatto
Federal University of Technology of Paraná
Curitiba, Paraná
Brazil

ISSN 1865-0929   ISSN 1865-0937 (electronic)
Communications in Computer and Information Science
ISBN 978-3-319-61402-1   ISBN 978-3-319-61403-8 (eBook)
DOI 10.1007/978-3-319-61403-8

Library of Congress Control Number: 2017945274

Printed on acid-free paper

This Springer imprint is published by Springer Nature
The registered company is Springer International Publishing AG
The registered company address is: Gewerbestrasse 11, 6330 Cham, Switzerland

Preface

Current communication systems cover a wide range of computing platforms, from traditional fixed telephony to mobile computing, multimedia systems, peer-to-peer Internet services, and critical embedded systems.

The research topics in embedded systems have increased and gained in importance. Consequently, communication between and among these systems has also increased, which has led to the emergence of new problems and challenges that need to be studied and tackled.

The interoperation of all these systems is a crucial characteristic. Integrating, connecting, and coordinating communication is fundamental for software and middleware systems.

Therefore, the Workshop on Communication in Critical Embedded Systems (WoCCES) focuses on important innovations and recent advances in the specification, design, construction, and use of communication in critical embedded systems. Its goal is to bring together researchers and practitioners from industry and academia and give them an opportunity to learn about the latest developments, deployments, technology trends, and research results as well as initiatives related to embedded systems and their applications in a variety of industrial environments.

This volume on "Special Issue on Communication of Critical Embedded Systems" in the Springer *Communications in Computer and Information Science* series (Springer CCIS) consists of the best papers selected from WoCCES 2013–2016, namely, the first, second, third, and fourth edition of the Workshop of Communication in Critical Embedded Systems.

WoCCES, which brings together researchers as well as undergraduate and graduate students of computer science, electrical engineering, mechatronics engineering, mechanical engineering, and related areas, is part of the most important Brazilian conference on Computer Networks and Distributed Systems (SBRC). Annually, WoCCES receives paper submissions that contribute to the high standard of SBRC providing updates on hot topics for researchers and enthusiasts of embedded systems and computer networks.

The Program Committee members are from around the world, and we have received and accepted papers from several different countries in previous editions. WoCCES is a special workshop that takes place in different Brazilian cities, and is also joined by renowned researchers as invited speakers. Although the call for papers is made available in both Brazilian Portuguese and English versions, the authors are encouraged to submit papers mainly in English aiming at increasing the international visibility of the event.

Previous WoCCES events comprised: the first edition (2013) in Brasília, Distrito Federal, Brazil, on May 10; the second edition (2014) in Florianópolis, Santa Catarina Brazil, on May 9; the third edition (2015) in Vitória, Espírito Santo, Brazil, May 22; and the fourth edition (2016) in Salvador, Bahia, Brazil, on June 3. All WoCCES editions were sponsored by the Brazilian Computer Society (SBC), with support from FAPs, CAPES, and CNPq.

We received 41 submissions, from which 24 papers were accepted. Each submitted paper was reviewed by at least three experts. The acceptance/rejection decision used the following criteria: All papers with two positive reviews were accepted, and those with two negative reviews were rejected. Borderline papers (with one positive and one negative review) were analyzed carefully by the conference chairs to evaluate the reasons given for acceptance or rejection. Our final decision on these submissions took into account mainly the potential of each paper to foster fruitful discussions and the future development of communication in critical embedded systems in the world, including those at initial stages. In some cases, one more review was carried out in order for a decision to be taken. The best papers were selected taking into consideration the best scores obtained by the papers according to the reviewers. We selected the 12 best papers from WoCCES 2013-2016. Extended and improved versions of the best papers were requested from the authors. The submitted papers were reviewed again by selected Program Committee members of the conferences and, after corrections, seven of these articles were accepted for publication in this volume of the CCIS series.

We would like to thank all the authors whose work and dedication made it possible to put together an exciting book and for their high-quality contributions. It is our hope that this Special Issue of the Springer CCIS volume will spark the interest of readers in these topics and motivate researchers all across the globe to intensify and extend their work in this field, as a solid basis for many more papers at future conferences. We are also enormously grateful to all Program Committee members and reviewers for their cooperation toward the success of this book.

We hope the papers will contribute to the development and evolution of this field, achieving a more realist balance between the communication and embedded system communities.

April 2017

Kalinka Branco
Alex Pinto
Daniel Pigatto

Organization

WoCCES 2013

General Chairs

Adriano Mauro Cansian	IBILCE – UNESP Rio Preto
Alex Sandro Roschildt Pinto	IBILCE – UNESP Rio Preto
José Márcio Machado	IBILCE – UNESP Rio Preto
Kalinka Regina Lucas Jaquie Castelo Branco	ICMC – USP, São Carlos
Paulo Henrique Moreira Gurgel	ICMC – USP, São Carlos

Program Committee

Edson dos Santos Moreira	ICMC-USP
Ellen Francine Barbosa	ICMC-USP
Marco Vieira	Universidade de Coimbra
Célia Leiko Ogawa Kawabata	IFSP - Instituto Federal de São Paulo - Campus São Carlos
Mário Meireles Teixeira	Universidade Federal do Maranhão
Marcos Fagundes Caetano	Universidade de Brasília
Jacir Luiz Bordim	Universidade de Brasília
Horácio Antonio Fernandes de Oliveira	Universidade Federal do Amazonas
João Cunha	Instituto Politécnico de Coimbra
Luciana Martimiano	Universidade Estadual de Maringá
Carlos Barros Montez	Universidade Federal de Santa Catarina
Mario Antonio Ribeiro Dantas	Universidade Federal de Santa Catarina
Raimundo Barreto	Universidade Federal do Amazonas
Luiz Henrique Castelo Branco	IFSP - Instituto Federal de São Paulo - Campus Araraquara
Paulo Portugal	Universidade do Porto (confirmado!)
Adriano Mauro Cansian	IBILCE - UNESP São José do Rio Preto
Alex Sandro Roschildt Pinto	IBILCE - UNESP São José do Rio Preto
José Márcio Machado	IBILCE - UNESP São José do Rio Preto
Kalinka Regina Lucas Jaquie Castelo Branco	ICMC-USP
Denis Fernando Wolf	ICMC-USP
Fernando Santos Osório	ICMC-USP
Fábio Dacêncio Pereira	UNIVEM
Angelo Passaro	IEA - Instituto de Estudos Avançados

WoCCES 2014

General Chairs

Adriano Mauro Cansian	IBILCE – UNESP Rio Preto
Alex Sandro Roschildt Pinto	IBILCE – UNESP Rio Preto
Daniel Fernando Pigatto	ICMC – USP, São Carlos
José Márcio Machado	IBILCE – UNESP Rio Preto
Kalinka Regina Lucas Jaquie Castelo Branco	ICMC – USP, São Carlos
Paulo Henrique Moreira Gurgel	ICMC – USP, São Carlos

Program Committee

Adriano Mauro Cansian	IBILCE - UNESP São José do Rio Preto
Alex Sandro Roschildt Pinto	IBILCE - UNESP São José do Rio Preto
Carlos Barros Montez	Universidade Federal de Santa Catarina
Célia Leiko Ogawa Kawabata	IFSP - Instituto Federal de São Paulo - Campus São Carlos
Daniel Fernando Pigatto	ICMC-USP
Denis Fernando Wolf	ICMC-USP
Edson dos Santos Moreira	ICMC-USP
Ellen Francine Barbosa	ICMC-USP
Fábio Dacêncio Pereira	UNIVEM
Fernando Santos Osório	ICMC-USP
Gustavo Pessin	Vale
Horácio Antonio Fernandes de Oliveira	Universidade Federal do Amazonas
Jacir Luiz Bordim	Universidade de Brasília
João Cunha	Instituto Politécnico de Coimbra
José Márcio Machado	IBILCE - UNESP São José do Rio Preto
Kalinka Regina Lucas Jaquie Castelo Branco	ICMC-USP
Luciana Martimiano	Universidade Estadual de Maringá
Luiz Henrique Castelo Branco	IFSP - Instituto Federal de São Paulo - Campus Araraquara
Marco Vieira	Universidade de Coimbra
Marcos Fagundes Caetano	Universidade de Brasília
Mario Antonio Ribeiro Dantas	Universidade Federal de Santa Catarina
Mário Meireles Teixeira	Universidade Federal do Maranhão
Paulo Portugal	Universidade do Porto
Raimundo Barreto	Universidade Federal do Amazonas

WoCCES 2015

General Chairs

Adriano Mauro Cansian	IBILCE – UNESP Rio Preto
Alex Sandro Roschildt Pinto	IBILCE – UNESP Rio Preto
Daniel Fernando Pigatto	ICMC - USP, São Carlos
Kalinka Regina Lucas Jaquie Castelo Branco	ICMC – USP, São Carlos
Paulo Henrique Moreira Gurgel	ICMC – USP, São Carlos

Program Committee

Adriano Mauro Cansian	IBILCE - UNESP São José do Rio Preto
Alex Sandro Roschildt Pinto	IBILCE - UNESP São José do Rio Preto
Carlos Barros Montez	Universidade Federal de Santa Catarina
Célia Leiko Ogawa Kawabata	IFSP - Instituto Federal de São Paulo - Campus São Carlos
Daniel Fernando Pigatto	ICMC-USP
Denis Fernando Wolf	ICMC-USP
Edson dos Santos Moreira	ICMC-USP
Ellen Francine Barbosa	ICMC-USP
Fábio Dacêncio Pereira	UNIVEM
Fernando Santos Osório	ICMC-USP
Gustavo Pessin	Vale
Horácio Antonio Fernandes de Oliveira	Universidade Federal do Amazonas
Jacir Luiz Bordim	Universidade de Brasília
João Cunha	Instituto Politécnico de Coimbra
Kalinka Regina Lucas Jaquie Castelo Branco	ICMC-USP
Luciana Martimiano	Universidade Estadual de Maringá
Luiz Henrique Castelo Branco	IFSP - Instituto Federal de São Paulo - Campus Araraquara
Marco Vieira	Universidade de Coimbra
Marcos Fagundes Caetano	Universidade de Brasília
Mario Antonio Ribeiro Dantas	Universidade Federal de Santa Catarina
Mário Meireles Teixeira	Universidade Federal do Maranhão
Paulo Portugal	Universidade do Porto
Raimundo Barreto	Universidade Federal do Amazonas

WoCCES 2016

General Chairs

Adriano Mauro Cansian	IBILCE – UNESP São José do Rio Preto
Alex Sandro Roschildt Pinto	UFSC-Blumenau
Daniel Fernando Pigatto	ICMC-USP, São Carlos
Kalinka Regina Lucas Jaquie Castelo Branco	ICMC-USP, São Carlos
Vandermi João da Silva	UFAM, Itacoatiara - Amazonas

Program Committee

Adriano Mauro Cansian	IBILCE – UNESP São José do Rio Preto
Alex Sandro Roschildt Pinto	UFSC-Blumenau
Carlos Barros Montez	UFSC
Célia Leiko Ogawa Kawabata	IFSP – Campus São Carlos
Daniel Fernando Pigatto	ICMC-USP
Denis Fernando Wolf	ICMC-USP
Edson dos Santos Moreira	ICMC-USP
Ellen Francine Barbosa	ICMC-USP
Fábio Dacêncio Pereira	UNIVEM
Fernando Santos Osório	ICMC-USP
Gustavo Pessin	Vale
Horácio Antonio Fernandes de Oliveira	UFAM
Ivanovitch Medeiros Dantas da Silva	IMD – Instituto Metropole Digital
Jacir Luiz Bordim	UNB
João Cunha	Instituto Politécnico de Coimbra
Kalinka Regina Lucas Jaquie Castelo Branco	ICMC-USP
Luciana Martimiano	UEM
Luiz Henrique Castelo Branco	IFSP – Campus Araraquara
Marco Vieira	Universidade de Coimbra
Marcos Fagundes Caetano	UNB
Mario Antonio Ribeiro Dantas	UFSC
Mário Meireles Teixeira	UFMA
Paulo Portugal	Universidade do Porto
Raimundo Barreto	UFAM
Rayner Pires de Melo	ICMC-USP
Vandermi João da Silva	UFAM

Special Issue CCIS Program Committee

Adriano Mauro Cansian	IBILCE - UNESP São José do Rio Preto
Alex Sandro Roschildt Pinto	Universidade Federal de Santa Catarina - Blumenau
Carlos Barros Montez	Universidade Federal de Santa Catarina
Carlos Silva Cardenas	Pontificia Universidad Catolica del Peru (Peru)
Célia Leiko Ogawa Kawabata	IFSP - Instituto Federal de São Paulo - Campus São Carlos
Daniel Fernando Pigatto	UTFPR Curitiba
Daniel Schneider	Fraunhofer Institute, Germany
Edson dos Santos Moreira	ICMC-USP
Ellen Francine Barbosa	ICMC-USP
Fábio Dacêncio Pereira	UNIVEM
Fernando Santos Osório	ICMC-USP
Gustavo Pessin	Vale Institute
Horácio Antonio Fernandes de Oliveira	Universidade Federal do Amazonas
Ivanovitch Medeiros Dantas da Silva	IMD - Instituto Metropole Digital
Jacir Luiz Bordim	Universidade de Brasília
Jean-Philippe Diguet	University of South Bregtane, France
Jim Smith	University of West of England, UK
João Cunha	Instituto Politécnico de Coimbra, Portugal
Jose R. Ortiz Ubarri	University of Puerto Rico, Puerto Rico
Kalinka Regina Lucas Jaquie Castelo Branco	ICMC-USP
Luciana Martimiano	Universidade Estadual de Maringá
Luiz Henrique Castelo Branco	IFSP - Instituto Federal de São Paulo - Campus Araraquara
Marco Vieira	Universidade de Coimbra, Portugal
Marcos Fagundes Caetano	Universidade de Brasília
Mario Antonio Ribeiro Dantas	Universidade Federal de Santa Catarina
Mário Meireles Teixeira	Universidade Federal do Maranhão
Martha Johanna	Inria departamento de Nanoeletrônica da Ecole Centrale em Lyon, France
Nicolas Laurie	ENAC - Ecole Nationale de l'Aviation Civile, Toulouse, France
Raimundo Barreto	Universidade Federal do Amazonas
Rayner Pires de Melo	ICMC-USP
Vandermi João da Silva	Universidade Federal do Amazonas
Yan Luo	University of Massachusetts Lowell, USA

Reviewers

Adriano Mauro Cansian	IBILCE - UNESP São José do Rio Preto
Alex Sandro Roschildt Pinto	Universidade Federal de Santa Catarina – Blumenau
Carlos Barros Montez	Universidade Federal de Santa Catarina – Florianópolis
Carlos Silva Cardenas	Pontificia Universidad Catolica del Peru, Peru
Célia Leiko Ogawa Kawabata	IFSP - Instituto Federal de São Paulo - Campus São Carlos
Daniel Fernando Pigatto	UTFPR Curitiba
Daniel Schneider	Fraunhofer Institute, Germany
Edson dos Santos Moreira	ICMC-USP
Ellen Francine Barbosa	ICMC-USP
Fábio Dacêncio Pereira	UNIVEM Marília
Fernando Santos Osório	ICMC-USP
Gustavo Pessin	Vale Institute
Horácio Antonio Fernandes de Oliveira	Universidade Federal do Amazonas
Ivanovitch Medeiros Dantas da Silva	IMD - Instituto Metropole Digital
Jacir Luiz Bordim	Universidade de Brasília (UNB)
Jean-Philippe Diguet	University of South Bregtane, France
Jim Smith	University of West of England, UK
João Cunha	Instituto Politécnico de Coimbra, Portugal
Jose R. Ortiz Ubarri	University of Puerto Rico, Puerto Rico
Kalinka Regina Lucas Jaquie Castelo Branco	ICMC-USP
Luciana Martimiano	Universidade Estadual de Maringá
Luiz Henrique Castelo Branco	IFSP - Instituto Federal de São Paulo - Campus Araraquara
Marco Vieira	Universidade de Coimbra
Marcos Fagundes Caetano	Universidade de Brasília (UNB)
Mario Antonio Ribeiro Dantas	Universidade Federal de Santa Catarina – Florianópolis
Mário Meireles Teixeira	Universidade Federal do Maranhão
Martha Johanna	Inria no departamento de Nanoeletrônica da Ecole Centrale em Lyon, France
Nicolas Laurie	ENAC - Ecole Nationale de l'Aviation Civile, Toulouse, France
Raimundo Barreto	Universidade Federal do Amazonas
Vandermi João da Silva	Universidade Federal do Amazonas
Yan Luo	University of Massachusetts Lowell, USA

Support Organizations

Critical Embedded System Laboratory – LSEC

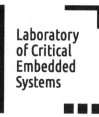

Publicity

SBC – Brazilian Computer Society

Financial Support

CNPq – National Council for Scientific and Technological Development
FAPESP – São Paulo Research Foundation

Contents

Experiments with XDense: A Dense Grid Sensor Network for Distributed Feature Extraction

João Loureiro$^{(\boxtimes)}$, Raghuraman Rangarajan, and Eduardo Tovar

CISTER/INESC-TEC, ISEP, Polytechnic Institute of Porto, Porto, Portugal
{joflo,raghu,emt}@isep.ipp.pt

Abstract. We propose XDense, a wired mesh grid sensor network architecture tailored for scenarios that benefit from thousands of sensors per square meter. XDense has a scalable network topology and protocol, customizable to application specifics, that enables complex feature extraction in realtime from the observed phenomena by exploiting the communication and distributed processing capabilities of such network topologies. We detail XDense's node and network architecture, protocols, and principles of operation. To demonstrate XDense's potentials, we evaluate it's response time, data traffic metrics and accuracy in the context of detecting fluid dynamic features.

1 Introduction

The advent of MEMS has enabled new applications to be developed that rely on dense deployments of sensors. In some applications, it has enabled deployments with very high spatial and temporal requirements. That is, resolutions as small as few micrometers of sensor inter space and sampling rates up to kHz. Application examples range from fluid mechanics for flow control in aircrafts [12], to artificial skins for robotics [29] and biomedical devices [24]. For such dense deployments, which may be of thousands of nodes in a few square meters area, sensor network technology faces scalability issues in some key aspects as such as cost, communication time, processing time, power, and reliability. For example, collecting data from the entire network can lead to a data explosion. Processing all this data for feature extraction becomes costly not only in terms of communication, but also computationally. Extraction may also be difficult to achieve in real time, hence prohibiting its use in real time critical applications like closed-loop actuation which leads to tight requirements.

We presented XDense as a mesh grid sensor network architecture, tailored to address the challenges of extremely dense sensor deployments [22]. It enables efficient extraction of complex features of the observed phenomena without the need of collecting the data from each individual node centrally. Instead, it allows the user to program node's feature detection and extraction algorithms with respect to the application's objectives. The data is processed in the network in a distributed fashion, and only meaningful data is delivered to the sink, thus reducing transmissions towards it, minimizing congestion, and leading to faster response times.

© Springer International Publishing AG 2017
K. Branco et al. (Eds.): WoCCES 2013-2016, CCIS 702, pp. 1–22, 2017.
DOI: 10.1007/978-3-319-61403-8_1

XDense moves away from traditional contention prone wireless and wired sensor network that uses shared medium to communicate. It resembles more closely Network-on-Chip (NoC) architectures. This is especially true regarding aspects like network topology (mesh grid based on regular structures), routing schemes, timing properties, and on the distributed processing opportunities associated [14]. On the other hand, we believe that the key differentiating features of our architecture are: (a) the network is not on a single chip, but built on a larger surface that is physically attached, specific to each application scenario (b) the node count is much greater than that of NoC applications, and (c) the network does not deal with shared memory due to a larger coverage area (which imposes different restrictions and opportunities).

Roadmap. We first conceptualized XDense with some preliminary simulation results [20], and demonstrated its implementability in hardware [21]. In [22] we provide a proof-of-concept on distributed feature extraction to detect turbulence in airflow data from computational fluid dynamics (CFD). In this paper, we expand on that proof-of-concept by adding two other simulation scenarios, featuring different data sources and distributed processing algorithms. We first perform feature detection on data from an image that captures a turbulent airflow. Following, we demonstrate the benefits on the network load due to performing in-network data compression, using CFD as the data source.

In the reminder of this paper we review the basics of the application requirements in Sect. 2, and then in Sect. 3, we describe the architecture and protocol specifics of the proposed system. In Sect. 4 we evaluate our experiments, and compare our work with traditional approaches for feature detection. In Sect. 5 we visit some related work from different domains that have inspired XDense. Finally in Sect. 6 presents the conclusions.

2   Dense Sensor Networks in Fluid Dynamics

An important objective in fluid dynamics is to characterize airflows and determine its laminar and turbulent characteristics. For example, in an aircraft, a high speed airflow over a wing can present both laminar and turbulent characteristics at the same time at different points of it. Turbulence can be highly undesirable on aircrafts since it increases drag and noise, and consequently fuel expended [2].

Figure 1 shows an airflow phenomena over a wing surface and illustrates the transition from laminar to turbulent flow. This transition delimits laminar flow (which has a more homogeneous speed profile distribution) from turbulent flows (which is composed of coherent structures, such as vortices of chaotic evolution) [27]. An increase in the turbulent region consequently increases drag on the surface of the wing, what makes fundamental to study flow's properties and understand its behavior.

There are various techniques available, to allow studying flows' properties by extracting profile data such as speed and temperature distribution [17]. For such profiles, large deployments of sensors may require sensors' inter-space to

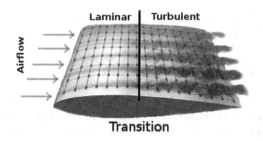

Fig. 1. Example scenario: air flow over a wing transiting from laminar to turbulent. We illustrate a potential deployment of XDense on the wing surface used to detect the transition region.

be smaller than that of the spatial granularity of the observed phenomena (for example, of 100 μm or less) and have high sampling rates (in excess of 10 kHz) [4]. Kasagi and others [12] surveyed micro flow sensors that attempt to meet such requirements. However, despite the effort gone towards sensor development, to the best of our knowledge, no interconnection solutions are found in the literature. Validations are usually done by individually connecting each sensor to channels of an analogue-to-digital converter (ADC) [3].

Another approach involves an imaging setup [32] to indirectly measure the speed distribution of an air-jet flow on free air using a camera and applying tracers on the flow. The authors proposed imaging processing algorithms to detect the boundary layer and turbulent structures. They extend their analysis in [31,33], and also provide statistical validation of their results. Great results for the boundary layer detection and quantification are also presented in [9–11] However, due to the dynamic and complex nature of the data in the above discussed approaches, data-processing is usually done offline and is limited to laboratory controlled conditions. This makes their use in real applications difficult.

Based on the above discussion, we state the following requirements of such a system, as being of interest to us, in sensing such phenomena in real time: (a) Efficient data extraction: The network infrastructure should allow efficient extraction of complex information about the phenomena. This should be done without the need of centralized data collection or processing. (b) Real time behaviour: Along with efficiency, the network infrastructure should also be able to respond in a timely manner such that actions can be taken based on the extracted data.

3 Proposed Architecture

The selection of a good topology is a job of fitting network requirements to available technology. A trade-off between cost and performance should always be considered when specifying many aspects, including connection density and length, and the number of IOs utilized for communication. Considering the requisites from Sect. 2, with the considerations above, we present our architecture in more detail in the following subsections.

3.1   Architecture

Network: The architecture consists of a 2D mesh network of sensor nodes and sinks, with point-to-point connections with up to four neighboring nodes, physically located in four directions (north, south, east, west). Figure 2(a) shows an example scenario of a 5 × 5 network (24 nodes and one sink) with the sink located in the center. Any set of nodes is a potential communication link from any node to the sink, enabling fault tolerant protocols. Multiple sinks are supported, and any node can be configured to be a sink while deploying and setting up and the network. Each node requires at least one sink in its address space to operate, but multiple sinks can be deployed to increase number addressable nodes (and network size), or to increase redundancy on data collection.

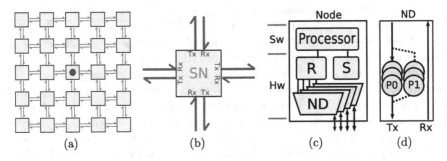

Fig. 2. (a) A 5 × 5 network with a sink in the center; (b) The node's pinout; (c) Node's model architecture: a Processor, a Router (R), the net-device (ND) and the sensor (S); (d) Net-device internals, with two queues with different priorities in the output channel (Tx), and the input channel on the right (Rx)

Node: Figure 2(c) shows the main functional blocks of a sensor node (*SN*). Each node can be seen as a system on chip (SoC), with dedicated hardware peripherals and a CPU. The Router (*R*) and the Net-Devices (*ND*) are responsible for communication on the network.[1] The Sensor (*S*) element is the interface with the physical world, and they are the sources of data. These peripherals are interconnected by the software layer, or application layer, which handles the communication protocol and the application specific algorithms.

---

[1] Our current implementation of a node is based on the Atmel ATSAM4N8A [1] microcontroller, which is a low power Cortex-M4-based processor, that runs at up to 100 MHz and features 512 KB of Flash and 64 KB of SRAM. Peripherals include five USARTs with DMA channel for fast serial communication, as well as an 12-bit ADCs.

The network is homogeneous and all nodes are capable of sensing, however the sinks have a backhaul link, that links the network with the exterior. This extra link can be, for example, to a wireless connection to a supervisory system, or to a local actuator interface, for closed loop actuation. Detailed information of each peripheral is provided in the sequence.

Net-Device: At the bottom layer in the node's architecture (Fig. 2(c)), Net-Devices (*ND*) are the node's hardware peripherals responsible for connecting two distinct nodes through the channel interface. Each node contains four *NDs* that connects them to their four immediate neighbors in the grid. It consists of a full-duplex serial port, with two fixed size output queues with different priorities. It's internal are in Fig. 2(d). Different queues are used for different protocols to minimize interference of one over the other. No input queues are used, since packets are processed immediately after being received.

Router: The router (*R*) is the interface between each *ND* and the Processor. It connects n *NDs* to the Processor and allows individual or parallel access to any *ND*. The router works on the basis of analysing the packet headers, and is able to not only send packets from the Processors to the *NDs*, but also it is able to store and forward packets between *NDs* independently from the Processor. This peripheral is ideally implemented using dedicated hardware for better response times. The packets have fixed size for the ease of processing by hardware.

Sensor: Another of the node's peripheral are the sensors, connected to the Processor through an analogue-to-digital interface. It is the network data input located at each node in the network. Each node can contain one or more sensors of any nature, according to the phenomena to be observed.

Processor: This where the user's applications and protocols run. It interfaces with the sensor, and implements high level communication primitives, and application-specific protocols for data sharing and processing on sensed data. In general, the application layer is responsible for reading from the sensor and deciding what to do with that information, and when, how and to whom to transmit its data through the net-devices. Another basic functionality is to enable the user to program all nodes in the network through a sink by broadcasting the new applications to this layer.

3.2   Application Scenario

Our application is designed using three operational states. Initially, all nodes wait until they receive a network discovery packet by the sink. After that, (i) each node collects and distributes its own sensor data within its neighborhood, (ii) processes the collected data, and depending on computed results and event detection algorithm policies, (iii) send its results to the closest known sink, in order to announce its findings. These operational states are named: *Network discovery*, *local data-sharing*, and *remote data-announcement* respectively, and

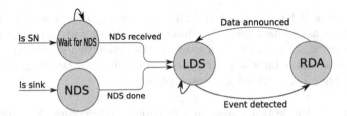

Fig. 3. Operational states of the network. The different operational states are: Network Discovery (NDS) or waiting for it, Local Data Sharing (LDS) and Remote Data Announcement (RDA).

from now on referred simply as *NDS*, *LDS* and *RDA*. Figure 3 is a diagram of the principles of operation. It shows each of the application operational states depending on node's role. The transitions represent the events that triggered the transition from one state to another.

Algorithm 1. Network discovery

---

1 **Function Begin()**
2   **if** $Self.IsSink = True$ **then**
3          $SinksList \leftarrow Self$
4          $Origin \leftarrow (0,0)$
5          $SerialNum+ = 1$
6          $Protocol \leftarrow NDS$
7          $Packet \leftarrow [Protocol, SerialNum, Origin]$
8          $SendPacket(Packet, AllDirections)$
9   **end**
10   **return**
11 **Function Received()**
12   **if** $Packet.Origin \notin SinksList$ **then**
13          $SinksList \leftarrow Packet.Origin$
14          $SendPacket(Packet, AllDirections \cap InputPort)$
15          $SwitchToLDS()$
16   **end**
17   **return**

Network Discovery (NDS): The Network discovery is executed once at initialization of the network by the sinks, which sends a single packet carrying the system's settings about sink location, baudrate, sampling rate, and the algorithms used for data processing. Nodes will wait for at least until they get an announcement from at least one sink, which is then added to the know sinks list. Algorithm 1 describes the execution of the *NDS* state from the sink and nodes side (source and destination). The $[x, y]$ coordinate pair (Line 4) are a relative address to the sink, that gets updated at each hop, such that it always reflect the position of the sink relative to the receiver of the packet. Each node forwards the packet to the neighboring nodes, except to the node where the packet came from. Redundant copies of the same packet can be received twice by the same node, in which case they are discarded (after comparing the serial number). After receiving and forwarding the packet for *NDS*, they switch to the next state (*LDS*).

Algorithm 2. Local Data Sharing

```
 1  Function Begin()
 2     if Self.IsSink = False then
 3         Origin ← (0,0)
 4         SerialNum+ = 1
 5         SensorValue ← ReadSensor()
 6         Protocol ← LDS
 7         Packet ← [Protocol, SerialNum, SensorValue, Origin]
 8         SensorsValueList ← Packet
 9         SendPacket(Packet, AllDirections)
10     end
11     return
12  Function Received()
13     if IsNew(Packet) then
14         if Packet ∉ SensorsValueList then
15             SensorsValueList ← Packet
16         end
17         else
18             SensorsValueList.Update(Packet)
19         end
20         if Distance(Packet.Origin) < MaxHops then
21             UpdateAddress(Packet.Origin, InputPort)
22             SendPacket(Packet, AllDirections ∩ InputPort)
23         end
24         if DetectEvents(SensorsValueList) = True then
25             SwitchToRDA()
26         end
27     end
28     return
```

***Local Data-Sharing* (LDS):** After receiving the announcement packet from the sink, the nodes continuously sense the environment for phenomena of interest. They communicate these sensed values with their neighborhood, of size defined by parameter n_{hops}. The neighborhood is a system defined parameter which plays an important role in the system operation. That is, all nodes initially send their values in all four directions, which is then stored and forwarded by the immediate neighboring nodes up to the n_{hops} neighbor.

The value of n_{hops} is selected according to the expected characteristics of the phenomena to observe, in such a way that, each node will send and receive data from up to N nodes around it. The greater the value of n_{hops}, the larger is the neighborhood N. This allows more detailed detections to be made but at the cost of increased overhead and latency. Using n_{hops}, the neighborhood size N is computed as the area of the lozenge neighborhood:

$$N = 4 \times \sum_{i=1}^{n_{hops}} i = 2 \times n_{hops} \times (n_{hops} + 1)$$

Algorithm 2 describes how the *LDS* state is started at each node, and how nodes deal with packets received from neighboring nodes. Basically, nodes receive data shared by their neighbors, store/refresh its value each time, forward it to other neighbors, and last, execute feature detection algorithms on the local data.

If after processing the data, the node detect a feature of interest, it immediately switches to the remote data-announcement (*RDA*) state and communicates its detection to the sink. Packets exchanged at the *LDS* state are queued in the lower priority queue *P0*.

Remote Data-Announcement (RDA): On switching to the *RDA* state, a node forwards the packet with information detected towards the closest sink. In turn, the sink receives announcements from different nodes, allowing it to reconstruct the observed phenomena with increasing accuracy and coverage as more announcements are received. Packets exchanged during this state are queued in the higher priority queue (*p1*). Algorithm 3 detail the execution of the *RDA* state by each node that have detected a feature of interest. Nodes transmit it to the sink and switch back to *LDS* state.

Algorithm 3. Remote Data Announcement

```
1  Function Announce()
2  │    Destination ← SinksList[0]
3  │    SerialNum+ = 1
4  │    Protocol ← RDA
5  │    Packet ← [Protocol, SerialNum, Event, Destination]
6  │    Port ← RouteTo(Destination)
7  │    SendPacket(Packet, Port)
8  │    SwitchToLDS()
9  │    return
10 Function Received()
11 │    if Packet.Destination ≠ (0, 0) then
12 │    │    UpdateAddress(Packet.Destination, InputPort)
13 │    │    Port ← RouteTo(Packet.Destination)
14 │    │    SendPacket(Packet, Port)
15 │    end
16 │    return
```

---

4   Evaluation

We want to evaluate XDense on fluid dynamic applications using different metrics. For that we define two sets of experiments: On the first, we are interested on verifying XDense accuracy on detecting the transition region between laminar and turbulent air-flow, running distributed edge detection algorithms, on different network configurations. Second, we want to identify the impact on XDense's performance by doing distributed data compression. We measure network workload, queue size and quality of extracted data, for different network configurations.

To perform the evaluation, we implemented our network using the Network Simulator 3 (NS-3) that implements all the abstraction of our architecture, for a matrix of sensor nodes with arbitrary parameters.[2]

Table 1 shows the system parameters that need to be configured. The SN deployment inter-space depends on the minimum size of the observed phenomena, and therefore has to be smaller than the minimum turbulent structure size [4]. The number of sensor nodes are chosen based on the area to be covered and we use a $101 \times 101 = 10201$ network with one sink in the center. The baudrate and sensor's sampling rate are also based on the application requirements and for this reason we normalize our temporal results to transmission time slots. A transmission time slot (TTS) is the time required to transmit one packet, or simply the packet duration.

Table 1. XDense simulation parameters.

Parameter	Value
Network dimension	101×101
Nodes	10200
Sinks	1
Neighbourhood size (n_{hops})	0 to 7
Baudrate	3 Mbps
Packet size	16 bytes
Packet duration (TTS)	53 μs

XDense packet structure was designed for low resource utilization and for ease of routing and processing by simple hardware. It uses 16 bytes size, which is a common UART buffer size on microcontrollers (μC), allowing easy handling of packets for increased reliability and decreased delays. Its structure is defined in Table 2.

The first byte is allocated for the communication protocol (P) and defines the routing protocol used, and hence determines how to interpret and use the

---

[2] It is an open source module for NS-3 that includes pre and post processing tools and simulator. The source code is available online at https://bitbucket.org/joaofl/noc.

Table 2. XDense packet structure

Field	Protocol	x_o	y_o	x_d	y_d	Payload	CS
Bytes	1	1	1	1	1	10	1

remaining content of packet's header. Two coordinate pair are used to specify origin (x_o, y_o) and destination (x_d, y_d) of the packet. If relative addressing scheme is used, origin and destination coordinates are updated at each hop, to maintain its relativity to the origin, otherwise kept fixed. Payload (PL) is used by the application layer to transmit sensed data, and any other application protocol required. Checksum (CS) is utilized for error checking.

Note that our aim is to analyze the performance of XDense and not the application performance per se (though we do present some results on its performance). Hence, the application of feature detection and clustering should only be considered as a demonstrator of XDense's performance for local distributed data processing.

4.1 Detecting the Transition Region on Image Data Source

In [31] the authors use a camera setup to indirectly measure the speed distribution of an air-jet flow on free air by applying tracers on the flow. They apply image processing techniques to detect such bounding interfaces on captured images. These processing techniques are applied sequentially on an image as follows: First, the image is binarized using a fixed threshold, then all the contours are traced, and finally, only the contour with the greatest area is chosen, with its indentations removed. This process is shown in Figs. 4(a) to (c). This image processing approach for feature detection is commonly used, and considering that our feature detection goals are the same, we use this approach as a reference to compare our results.

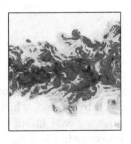  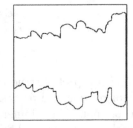

(a) Original image   (b) Binarization and contour tracing   (c) Contour smoothing

Fig. 4. Process steps for boundary computation described in [31].

We do that as follows: first, we use the same flow image from [31] as an input to our XDense simulation (this is, the data is superimposed in the simulation of our sensor network grid, and is sampled by each node's sensor). We detect the transition region envelope, which is then compared with the envelope previously computed by processing the same snapshot, and applying the processing steps from [31]. Comparing the two results gives us a measure of the accuracy of our computation. We utilize an adaptation of the Sobel operator for edge detection [30], widely used the image processing domain. Using this algorithm, nodes performs a 2-D spatial gradient measurement on it's neighboring data, and so emphasizes regions of high spatial frequency that correspond to edges.

Figure 5 summarizes graphically the results of our simulation using $n_{size} = 3$. It shows the original snapshot (Fig. 5(a)), the events detected by XDense nodes (Fig. 5(b)), and the resulting bounding interface (Fig. 5(c)) superimposed with the contour smoothing, done with image processing technique (original output from Fig. 4(c)). Figures 6 and 7 show (a) the detected transition by the SNs and (b) the calculated envelope by the sink. The images allow visual comparison that support our numerical results, and provides the intuition for the impact on the accuracy of the detection algorithm by varying the neighborhood size ($n_{size} = 1$ and 7).

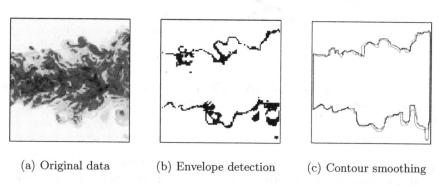

(a) Original data   (b) Envelope detection   (c) Contour smoothing

Fig. 5. Processing steps of our network. (a) Is the phenomena as seem by our network, after downsampling the full resolution image to 101×101 pixels. (b) is the transition envelope detection by the SNs with $n_{hops} = 3$, and (c) is the contour smoothing post processing done by the sink in black, superimposed on 4(c).

Using this process, we evaluate the behavior of our system under varying neighborhood size (n_{hops}). We are interested in observing: (i) the accuracy of our bounding interface detection; (ii) the total number of transmissions and (iii) the total time needed to acquire this bounding interface. We then compare it to centralized data acquisition approach.

The cumulative distribution function (CDF) in Fig. 8 gives a measure of the effect of dimensioning different system parameters (density, neighborhood size). Figure 8 shows that for $2 < n_{hops} < 4$, more that 80% of the snapshot has an error under 3%. Moreover, increasing neighborhood size does not necessarily

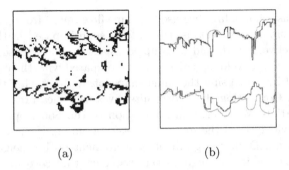

Fig. 6. Processing steps of our network. (a) Transition envelope detection by the SNs with $n_{hops} = 1$, and (b) is the contour smoothing post processing done by the sink in black, superimposed on 4(c).

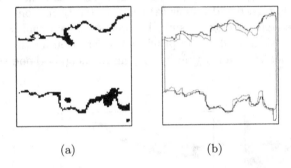

Fig. 7. Processing steps of our network. (a) Transition envelope detection by the SNs with $n_{hops} = 7$, and (b) is the contour smoothing post processing done by the sink in black, superimposed on 4(c).

implies in greater accuracy, but in smaller number of detections. The other way around, the minimum neighborhood size ($n_{hops} = 1$) presents noisy detections, and an intermediate values of n_{hops} might provide the best trade-off. This results are enforced by the analysis of Figs. 5, 6 and 7. Small neighborhoods add great granularity to the edge detection, but adds noise on contour smoothing. In the other hand, larger neighborhoods may introduce errors on the edge detection, but gives a more consistent contour smoothing.

Figure 9(a) shows the trade-off between the maximum end-to-end delay in terms of transmission time slots (TTS), and mean square error (MSE) of the envelope found. This gives an idea of how responsiveness varies for the different values of n_{hops}, and the impact on the accuracy. With $n_{hops} = 3$ MSE is minimum, with a minimum cost in time, when compared to $n_{hops} = 2$ which presents the best response time, but with higher MSE. Figure 9(b) presents the number of transmissions, therefore providing a picture of the actual load on the network. It shows that, with increase in neighborhood size, the number of global transmissions (DA) goes down (although the local transmissions (DS) increases

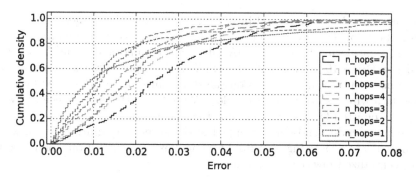

Fig. 8. Cumulative density function for different values of n_{hops}, of the error between the reference envelope, and the detected envelope.

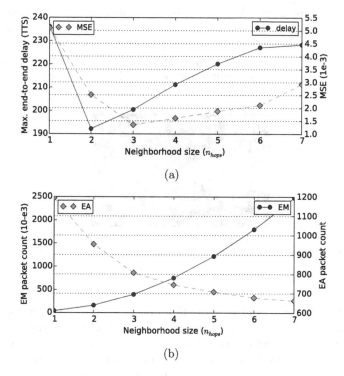

(a)

(b)

Fig. 9. (a) Trade-off between mean square error (MSE) and maximum end-to-end delay (TTS) for different values of n_{hops}, and (b) is the total number of transmissions for the different protocols, for the same values of n_{hops}

accordingly). This in turn affects the total transmissions time (as can be seen back in Fig. 9(a)).

To give an idea of the responsiveness scales of our system, we compare it with an hypothetical scenario with the same deployment, in which the sink reads all the nodes centrally using shared buses. Each bus would be connected to one of the four ports of the sink, in such a way that each bus covers a quadrant of the network. Considering perfect TDMA, all the four quadrants could be read in parallel, in $(101 \times 101 - 1)/4 = 2550$ TTS. This corresponds to the time required to each node to transmit it's data on the shared medium, as in shared buses or in standard wireless links (at this scales). We refer to this as the scenario with $n_{hops} = 0$, omitted from some plots due to scaling issues.

Maximum end-to-end delay dropped in the order of magnitude of 10, when distributed data processing is utilized for complex data extraction, compared to simple centralized raw data extraction.

4.2 Distributed Data Compression from CFD Data

On our second experiment, instead of using the flow image as our data input, we use data from Computation Fluid Dynamics (*CFD*). This is, we simulate a similar scenario of an air-jet flow on free air, but using *CDF* data from [6], to "feed" our simulator (instead of using data from a picture). Figure 10 shows the *CFD* data representation, superimposed by the XDense network.

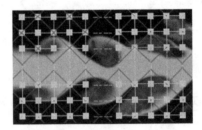

Fig. 10. XDense network superimposed on the CFD dataset snapshot from [6], showing clustering for $n_{hops} = 1$.

The metrics collected in the evaluation are for analyzing the performance of XDense and help in evaluating dimensioning issues. We analyze the performance of XDense in terms of end-to-end delay, load on the network, queue size and quality of acquired data. Nodes operate synchronously, which means that all the nodes initiate *LDS* in parallel, leading to peaks of network activity, and to a stress condition that we study.

Extracting data from all the nodes in the network is useful for many application scenarios and also for system design decisions. The simplest XDense setup for this purpose is for all nodes to transmit all sensed information to the sink. Intuitively, depending on the load an application scenario places on the XDense network, this may not be a suitable approach. Data aggregation and compression techniques then need to be evaluated.

In this subsection, we evaluate XDense performance in reading all data either directly or with some form of local distributed data processing technique (like clustering and data aggregation). The aim is to find a balance between local data sharing (LDS) and aggregation and remote data announcements to the sink (in the RDA state).

For data aggregation, we use Least Square Regression [7]. This is a simple data fitting algorithm, suitable and used in embedded devices applications. It demonstrates data aggregation for significant gains in performance. As discussed before, there are many other possible approaches depending on the application scenario, and we use these only as a place holder to demonstrate XDense. In this experiment, we use the nearest Source-like clustering algorithm to perform clustering [13].

We now describe both these functions briefly. For clustering, in the NDS state, each node verifies three conditions related to its location and neighborhood size (n_{hops}) in order to perform leader election:

$$\begin{cases} x \bmod n_{hops} = 0 \\ y \bmod n_{hops} = 0 \\ (x+y) \bmod (2 \times n_{hops}) = 0 \end{cases} \tag{1}$$

If satisfied, the node tags itself as cluster head and a cluster is formed. Figure 10 illustrates this for $n_{hops} = 1$; the lozenge shaped areas are clusters with leader being the node in the center. In the LDS state, each leader receives data from its neighbors and performs data aggregation by fitting a plane (of shape $z = ax + by + c$) to the data of its N neighbors. Least square regression is used to provide the best fit for the data points, by minimizing the distances between the points (xi, yi, zi) and the plane. In the RDA state, the calculated data is announced to the sink with the values of $a, b, c.$ and the curve type index.

Figure 11(a) shows the number of transmissions over transmission time slots (TTS) for different values of n_{hops}, which is the load on the network for that specific data snapshot. For $n_{hops} > 0$, a maximum load spike in the beginning is caused by the LDS state (shown in Fig. 11(b)). This maximum load increases with increase in n_{hops}. Figure 11(b) zooms in on transmission until $t = 55$, showing the drop as nodes switch from LDS to RDA. Comparing $n_{hops} = 1$ and 4, this trade-off is seen between increasing LDS and decreasing number of RDA transmissions.

A qualitative comparison of output data, for different values of n_{hops}, can be done by analyzing Fig. 13. For $n_{hops} = 0$, all nodes transmit their readings and this is the maximum possible resolution of the phenomena achievable with our deployment. Intuitively, greater the n_{hops} value, the greater is the data loss due to errors while fitting a plane to the data-set. Figure 15 shows the balance between total number of LDS and RDA transmissions for different values of n_{hops}.

We also check the impact of neighborhood cluster sizes on end-to-end delay and accuracy of acquired data when varying n_{hops} sizes. Figure 14 shows a quantitative comparison of the trade-off between error and maximum end-to-end delay. Accuracy is measured with the mean square error (MSE) of the sum of

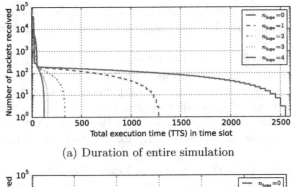

(a) Duration of entire simulation

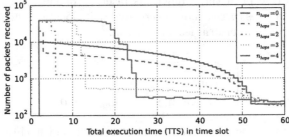

(b) Zoom in on the transmission time interval (0 to 60)

Fig. 11. Reading sensed data: number of receptions over time for different values of n_{hops}.

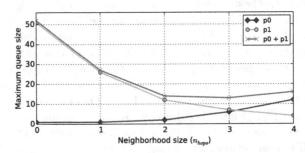

Fig. 12. Reading sensed data: maximum queue size for $n_{hops} = 1$ to 4.

differences between data for scenarios, with n_{hops} varying from 1 to 5, from the best possible case (which is $n_{hops} = 0$).

The MSE grows with increasing n_{hops}, while maximum end-to-end delay decreases. Looking at these results, $n_{hops} = 2$ seems to be a good choice, since the smaller turbulent structures are still distinguishable and it represents a reduction in the maximum end-to-end delay of approximately 75% of the worst case scenario. With increasing n_{hops}, better curve fitting algorithms could lead to a smaller slope of the error but the trend will remain the same.

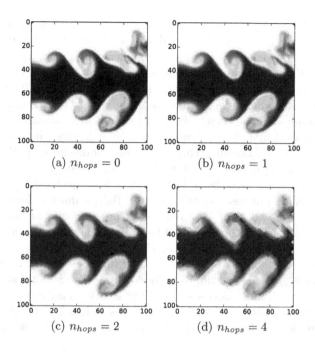

Fig. 13. Reading sensed data: extracted data for different values of n_{hops}.

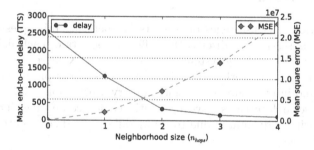

Fig. 14. Reading sensed data: trade-off between mean square error and maximum end-to-end delay for different values of n_{hops}.

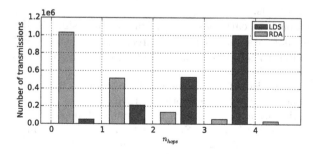

Fig. 15. Total number of packets transmitted in the network with $n_{hops} = 1$ to 4.

Figure 12 shows the maximum queue size on the network for the different values of n_{hops}, for both queues $p0$ and $p1$ (used for LDS and RDA packets respectively). $p1$ queue size is greater for smaller values of n_{hops}, since greater the number of $RDAs$ greater is the congestion towards the sink. However, there is a peak for $n_{hops} = 1$, showing that the introduction of the LDS state (absent for $n_{hops} = 0$), introduces congestion. Because, even with $p1$ having priority over $p0$, our model is non-preemptive, and to serve $p1$, a transmission from $p0$ has to be completed first. The $p0$ queue size also increases with the increase in neighborhood size. Additionally, while not shown, nodes in the path to the sink suffer from increasing queues, as all packets compete for paths leading to the sink. The closer a node is to the sink, the longer is its queue size.

We can compare our results with Pressure Belt, a master-slave, shared bus based network proposed in [8], for monitoring pressure over an aircraft wing.[3] The authors calculate the time required to read all the nodes simply as: *number of nodes × packet duration*. Normalizing Pressure Belt results, and considering one master for each quarter of all nodes, Pressure Belt would have the same performance of $n_{hops} = 0$ scenario. But, due to physical and electrical limitations, and due to the maximum address space, their solution may not be suitable for this density of nodes. Moreover, their solution was designed for offline processing, acting as a simple data logger, making it inapplicable for real-time applications.

5 Related Work

For its operation, XDense relies on subsets of operating principles of distinct systems. In this section we discuss the different aspects of each field that we consider in our work and the systems that are close to XDense.

For example, our network architecture resembles Array processors [16] that are widely found in literature and inside industry. Both application specific and general propose architectures have been utilized for computing. This kind of architecture brings advantages due to its modularity and scalability (based on regular structures).

Although specific implementations are generally done to address specific problems. For each kind of processor, different network topologies are utilized to interconnect its processing elements, whereas the topology is chosen according to the application goals.

For example, back on early 80s, grids of processors using VLSI were explored to perform relational database operations directly in hardware [15]. Each processing element is suited to compare tuples of data, but when combined can perform

---

[3] Pressure Belt [8] consists of a strip mounted crosswise on the wing of an aircraft, connected in one extremity to a coordinator, and has an embedded data-logger situated inside the airplane. It runs over two parallel full-duplex RS485 shared links, compatible with the IEEE 1451.2 Standard for a Smart Transducer Interface for Sensors and Actuators. Up to 255 nodes can communicate at 5 Mbps with packets of 48 bits each. By using a clock synchronization scheme, time division multiple access (TDMA) is used to communicate with the nodes.

complex database operations. Geometric-arithmetic Parallel Processor (GAPP) is a parallel processor with over 10,000 processing elements [5]. It consisted of very simple processing elements (one bit sum only) to perform matrix operations for image processing in military applications, like tracking targets. Although the interconnection arrangement is similar to our work, the processing elements are passive, and are not a network of active programmable nodes as conceived for our design. Grid networks of more complex processors have now become commercially available [25] and allow complex distributed data processing algorithms to explore the many-core computational potentials in a transparent way.

Our work has similarities to boundary estimation and tracking techniques using collaborative sensors found in literature, and a good review of such techniques can be found in [28]. Many of such techniques often construct an hierarchical structure, and apply data aggregation functions as the data travels up the hierarchy. Other works (e.g. [18]), employ techniques that, similarly to us, rely on local communication between neighbours to detect contours, however were projected for shared medium link layers, and opportunities are limited due to concurrency issues.

Wireless sensor networks (WSN) are suitable for large scale deployments, and effort have gone towards minimizing communication by distributively processing data. For example, in [23], the authors explore distributed data compression. Although wireless sensor nodes exceed in complexity, power constraints, size, latency and overhead, and therefore does not meet the application temporal requirements.

Closer to our architecture, a multi modal sensor network was proposed in [19]. The authors present a sensor network with an embedded processor dedicated to each sensor node. Node communicate using an infrared transceiver, with its surrounding neighbors, using a single full-duplex serial. The authors presents a scalable sensor network deployment and propose solutions for data management, localization, data aggregation and routing. But, due to link contentions and collisions, in other words, cost of communication, their research leans more towards WSNs, which are not suitable for the applications we are focused on. The concept was extended, and an alternative topologies were presented in [26]. Although the network is a wired grid, master-slave communication is utilized, decreasing distributed processing opportunities due to shared links. The number of slaves is also limited, which is not scalable.

6   Conclusion

Dense sensor networks, like our proposed XDense, are going to be increasingly used in application scenarios which require realtime data. Combined with novel feature detection techniques systems can then recreate the phenomena, present in the application scenarios, and use this information for actuations. We evaluated the XDense architecture and protocols work with performance metrics on accuracy, timeliness and network usage and showed the tradeoffs that have to be made among the parameters (such as, larger neighborhood leads to increased accuracy but also increased traffic). It is important to understand the underlying issues that affect the performance of XDense. One issue is that of dimensioning XDense based on the requirements imposed by the application scenario. We showed that dimensioning issues such as node density and neighborhood size affect the performance of the system and depend closely on the application scenario.

We use a simple and deadlock free flooding mechanism but results in an excessive number of redundant transmissions in a scenario in which the network activity is very high (considering that all the remaining nodes may be operating in the same state). Alternative routing protocols should be implemented in order to decrease redundancy, and consequently, the network utilization and total latency (addressed in parallel work [22]).

Another issue are the feature detection techniques which strongly affects the performance. We used one base technique for evaluation and we intend to investigate further techniques for comparative analysis. It is important to note that the simplicity of the algorithms utilized, allow for practical construction of such networks using currently technology, as demonstrated earlier in [21]. For example, with COTS microcontrollers or a SoC solution could be developed for it, to be low cost.

Acknowledgments. This work was partially supported by National Funds through FCT/MEC (Portuguese Foundation for Science and Technology) and when applicable, co-financed by ERDF (European Regional Development Fund) under the PT2020 Partnership, within project UID/CEC/04234/2013 (CISTER Research Centre); also by FCT/MEC and ERDF through COMPETE (Operational Programme 'Thematic Factors of Competitiveness'), within project FCOMP-01-0124-FEDER-020312 (SMART-SKIN); by FCT/MEC and the EU ARTEMIS JU within project ARTEMIS/0004/2013 - JU grant nr. 621353 (DEWI, www.dewi-project.eu); by the government of Brazil through CNPq, Conselho Nacional de Desenvolvimento Científico e Tecnológico.

References

1. Atmel. http://www.atmel.com/devices/sam4n8a
2. Blake, W.K.: Mechanics of Flow-Induced Sound and Vibration V2: Complex Flow-Structure Interactions, vol. 2. Elsevier, Amsterdam (2012)
3. Bruinink, C., Jaganatharaja, R., de Boer, M., Berenschot, E., Kolster, M., Lammerink, T., Wiegerink, R., Krijnen, G.: Advancements in technology and design of biomimetic flow-sensor arrays. In: IEEE 22nd International Conference on Micro Electro Mechanical Systems, MEMS 2009, pp. 152–155, January 2009
4. Buder, U., Petz, R., Kittel, M., Nitsche, W., Obermeier, E.: Aeromems polyimide based wall double hot-wire sensors for flow separation detection. Sens. Actuators A: Phys. **142**(1), 130–137 (2008)
5. Cloud, E.: The geometric arithmetic parallel processor. In: Proceedings of the 2nd Symposium on the Frontiers of Frontiers of Massively Parallel Computation, pp. 373–381, October 1988
6. da Silva, C.B., Pereira, J.C.: Invariants of the velocity-gradient, rate-of-strain, rate-of-rotation tensors across the turbulent/nonturbulent interface in jets. Phys. Fluids (1994-present) **20**(5), 055101 (2008)

7. Datta, B.N.: Numerical Linear Algebra and Applications. SIAM, Philadelphia (2010)
8. Gen-Kuong, F., Swanson, B.: Network sensor systems- the pressure belt application. In: 19th Aerospace Testing Seminar, Manhattan Beach, CA, pp. 379–390 (2000)
9. Haller, G.: Lagrangian coherent structures from approximate velocity data. Phys. Fluids (1994-present) **14**(6), 1851–1861 (2002)
10. Haller, G., Yuan, G.: Lagrangian coherent structures and mixing in two-dimensional turbulence. Physica D: Nonlinear Phenom. **147**(3), 352–370 (2000)
11. Holzner, M., Liberzon, A., Guala, M., Tsinober, A., Kinzelbach, W.: Generalized detection of a turbulent front generated by an oscillating grid. Exp. Fluids **41**(5), 711–719 (2006)
12. Kasagi, N., Suzuki, Y., Fukagata, K.: Microelectromechanical systems-based feedback control of turbulence for skin friction reduction. Annu. Rev. Fluid Mech. **41**, 231–251 (2009)
13. Krishnamachari, B., Estrin, D., Wicker, S.: The impact of data aggregation in wireless sensor networks. In: Proceedings of the 22nd International Conference on Distributed Computing Systems Workshops, pp. 575–578 (2002)
14. Kumar, S., Jantsch, A., Soininen, J.-P., Forsell, M., Millberg, M., Oberg, J., Tiensyrja, K., Hemani, A.: A network on chip architecture and design methodology. In: Proceedings of the IEEE Computer Society Annual Symposium on VLSI 2002, pp. 105–112. IEEE (2002)
15. Kung, H.T., Lehman, P.L.: Systolic (VLSI) arrays for relational database operations. In: Proceedings of the 1980 ACM SIGMOD International Conference on Management of Data, SIGMOD 1980, pp. 105–116. ACM, New York (1980)
16. Kung, S.Y.: VLSI array processors. Englewood Cliffs, NJ, Prentice Hall, 1988, 685 p. Research supported by the Semiconductor Research Corp., SDIO, NSF, and US Navy., vol. 1 (1988)
17. LaRue, J.C.: Detection of the turbulent-nonturbulent interface in slightly heated turbulent shear flows. Phys. Fluids (1958–1988) **17**(8), 1513–1517 (1974)
18. Li, M., Liu, Y.: Iso-map: energy-efficient contour mapping in wireless sensor networks. IEEE Trans. Knowl. Data Eng. **22**(5), 699–710 (2010)
19. Lifton, J., Seetharam, D., Broxton, M., Paradiso, J.: Pushpin computing system overview: a platform for distributed, embedded, ubiquitous sensor networks. In: Mattern, F., Naghshineh, M. (eds.) Pervasive 2002. LNCS, vol. 2414, pp. 139–151. Springer, Heidelberg (2002). doi:10.1007/3-540-45866-2_12
20. Loureiro, J., Gupta, V., Pereira, N., Tovar, E., Rangarajan, R.: XDense: a sensor network for extreme dense sensing. In: Proceedings of the Work-In-Progress Session at the 2013 IEEE Real-Time Systems Symposium - RTSS, pp. 19–20 (2013)
21. Loureiro, J., Rangarajan, R., Tovar, E.: Demo abstract: towards the development of XDense, a sensor network for dense sensing. In: 12th European Conference on Wireless Sensor Networks - EWSN, p. 23 (2015)
22. Loureiro, J., Rangarajan, R., Tovar, E.: Distributed sensing of fluid dynamic phenomena with the XDense sensor grid network. In: 2015 IEEE 3rd International Conference on Cyber-Physical Systems, Networks, and Applications (CPSNA), pp. 54–59, August 2015
23. Luo, C., Wu, F., Sun, J., Chen, C.W.: Compressive data gathering for large-scale wireless sensor networks. In: Proceedings of the 15th Annual International Conference on Mobile Computing and Networking, pp. 145–156. ACM (2009)
24. Ohta, J., Tokuda, T., Sasagawa, K., Noda, T.: Implantable CMOS biomedical devices. Sens. (Basel, Switzerland) **9**(11), 9073 (2009)

25. Olofsson, A., Nordström, T., Ul-Abdin, Z.: Kickstarting high-performance energy-efficient manycore architectures with epiphany. In: 2014 48th Asilomar Conference on Signals, Systems and Computers, pp. 1719–1726. IEEE (2014)
26. Paradiso, J.A., Lifton, J., Broxton, M.: Sensate media-multimodal electronic skins as dense sensor networks. BT Technol. J. **22**(4), 32–44 (2004)
27. Robinson, S.K.: Coherent motions in the turbulent boundary layer. Annu. Rev. Fluid Mech. **23**(1), 601–639 (1991)
28. Srinivasan, S., Dattagupta, S., Kulkarni, P., Ramamritham, K.: A survey of sensory data boundary estimation, covering and tracking techniques using collaborating sensors. Pervasive Mob. Comput. **8**(3), 358–375 (2012)
29. Takei, K., Takahashi, T., Ho, J.C., Ko, H., Gillies, A.G., Leu, P.W., Fearing, R.S., Javey, A.: Nanowire active-matrix circuitry for low-voltage macroscale artificial skin. Nat. Mater. **9**(10), 821–826 (2010)
30. Vincent, O., Folorunso, O.: A descriptive algorithm for sobel image edge detection. In: Proceedings of Informing Science & IT Education Conference (InSITE), pp. 97–107 (2009)
31. Westerweel, J., Fukushima, C., Pedersen, J.M., Hunt, J.: Momentum and scalar transport at the turbulent/non-turbulent interface of a jet. J. Fluid Mech. **631**, 199–230 (2009)
32. Westerweel, J., Hofmann, T., Fukushima, C., Hunt, J.: The turbulent/non-turbulent interface at the outer boundary of a self-similar turbulent jet. Exp. Fluids **33**(6), 873–878 (2002)
33. Westerweel, J., Petracci, A., Delfos, R., Hunt, J.C.: Characteristics of the turbulent/non-turbulent interface of a non-isothermal jet. Philos. Trans. R. Soc. A: Math. Phys. Eng. Sci. **369**(1937), 723–737 (2011)

Performance Evaluation of Handoff in Mobile IPv6 Networks: The Case of Safety-Critical Systems with NIMBLE Platform for Mobility

Lucas Tognoli Munhoz, Daniel F. Pigatto[(⊠)],
and Kalinka Regina Lucas Jaquie Castelo Branco

Universidade de São Paulo (USP), Avenida Trabalhador São-carlense, 400,
São Carlos, SP 13566-590, Brazil
lucas.munhoz@usp.br, danielpigatto@gmail.com

Abstract. In real-time systems, when failures of any nature come to happen, high-value assets are put at risk and in some cases even human lives. Due to this high criticality, developing improvements to these systems in order to increase their safety becomes a topic of high importance. This research reviews handoff procedures in IPv6 networks to help identify those with lower latency and low packet loss during the operation, aiming to increase the efficiency of general communication in these systems. For this, some handoff techniques found in the literature are simulated and, from the obtained results, performance comparisons are presented following specific statistical techniques to evaluate the performance of computational systems. Finally, a discussion on the application of these techniques in critical embedded systems is presented, specially unmanned vehicles.

Keywords: Handover · Handoff · Mobile IPv6 · Safety-critical vehicles · Unmanned vehicles

1 Introduction

In the last few years there has been a growing interest in Unmanned Vehicles (UV) and Unmanned Systems, leading to the co-existence of many different types of vehicles e.g. aerial, terrestrial and aquatic vehicles. These systems should be integrated into the airspace, on public roads or on aquatic environments following specific laws and requirements of each scenario, mainly related to safety. Thus, it is essential that communications carefully meet mobility and time requirements, increasing the system overall capabilities and, consequently, allowing these vehicles to be certified and integrated into their operation space.

UVs are becoming highly connected for cooperation purposes (e.g. distributed tasks), and also to the Internet for real-time services provision (e.g. IoT and cloud-based applications). Thus, a tendency on these areas is the use of IPv6 protocol that allows an exclusive address on the Internet and provides mobility approaches suitable for UVs applications.

© Springer International Publishing AG 2017
K. Branco et al. (Eds.): WoCCES 2013-2016, CCIS 702, pp. 23–44, 2017.
DOI: 10.1007/978-3-319-61403-8_2

Therefore, the study of handoff process on IPv6 is an important research topic for applications that depend on wireless mobile networks, mainly due to the fact that it is a critical aspect regarding connection quality that is impacted by packet losses during handoff transition process. Thus, it is necessary to analyse how worth the handoff process is considering network conditions (there might exist a better network to choose to connect to) and the criticality of an ongoing operation. Moreover, when it comes to high critical applications, handoff might be a failure point to be considered.

The goal of this paper is to compare two handoff algorithms in IPv6 networks, especially investigating the impact of mobility support. Our contributions extend to embedded systems connected by IPv6 mobile networks, providing data and comparisons that can be used by developers and researchers. We analyse aspects such as run time in each step of the process and factors that influence the decision-making algorithm, such as signal strength and data transmission rate.

The overall organisation of this paper is: Sect. 2 presents the state of the art with related works that identify the gap addressed by this paper; Sect. 3 details the Internet Protocol version 6; Sect. 4 introduces a data communication architecture and emphasises the NIMBLE platform for mobility which was proposed for safety-critical unmanned systems; Sect. 5 provides an explanation about techniques used for results treatment; Sect. 6 demonstrates the simulations experimental setup; Sect. 7 presents results and discussions; Sect. 8 connects results and discussions to the UVs field; and, finally, Sect. 9 concludes the paper.

2   Background

The advantage of wireless mesh networks is seen when self-organisation is coupled with seamless handover to provide continuity of service to the users. Handover (sometimes seen as handoff) is common in cellular networks, where mobile stations frequently move out of the coverage area of one cell tower and into that of a neighbouring tower [7].

In [15], authors measured latencies of all handoff process stages. They concluded that: (i) the wireless network adapter used in both the Mobile Unit (MU) and the Access Points (APs) directly influences the handoff latency; (ii) different MUs treat sequences of messages slightly different; and (iii) the search phase takes about 90% of the handoff process time. However, authors did not explore real situations even with simulated results, which might change the perception if contextualised in some areas.

In [27], authors discussed the effects of handoff in data transmission. Similarly to [15], they concluded that the network interface affects latency, and the longest stage of the process is search. They have also noted that a MU can keep receiving data from previously connected AP even during the search phase. Finally, authors concluded that the behavior of handoff process depends not only on the hardware used (network adapter), but also on data stream, e.g., if MU is sending or receiving packets.

In [4], authors discussed latency issues in Mobile IPv6 and its derivative PMIPv6, highlighting the difficulty of using such handoff mechanisms in real-time systems. To solve this problem, authors proposed a new handoff scheme for PMIPv6 network that reduces latency and solves the loss problem.

We have identified that there is a lack of comparisons between IPv6 protocol with and without mobility on the context of unmanned aerial vehicles (UAVs). Thus, this paper will carry out a discussion on how handoff process impacts IPv6 networks from the point of view of unmanned aircraft systems (UAS) in general, which includes not only the UAV, but all the supporting systems.

Next section will address important concepts review on IPv6.

3   Internet Protocol Version 6

In 1990s, the Internet Engineering Task Force (IETF) started developing the successor to the IPv4 protocol. The motivation for that was the fact that 32-bit IP address was beginning to be used up as more devices were connected to the Internet with unique IP addresses. To respond for the need of a large IP address space, a new IP protocol was developed. The Internet Protocol version 6 (IPv6) has also improved some aspects based on accumulated operational experience with IPv4 [12]. There was considerable debate about when the IPv4 addresses would be completely allocated. Many approaches were developed since then trying to prolong the use of IPv4 as much as possible. However, we have been currently seeing major companies and institutions moving to IPv6, but the transition may still take some time to be fully completed.

According to [12], the most important changes in IPv6 datagram (Fig. 1) format are:

- **Expanded addressing capabilities.** IPv6 increases the size of the IP address from 32 to 128 bits, ensuring that there will be enough IP addresses for nowadays applications. As a comparison matter, every grain of sand on the planet can be IP-addressable.
- **A streamlined 40-byte header.** The 40-byte fixed-length header allows for faster processing of the IP datagram. A new encoding of options allows for more flexible options processing.
- **Flow labelling and priority.** IPv6 has an elusive definition of a flow e.g. audio and video transmission might likely be treated as a flow. On the contrary, the more traditional applications might not be treated as flows. Thus, the designers of IPv6 foresee the eventual need to be able to differentiate among the flows.

The following fields are defined in IPv6 [12] (see Fig. 1):

- **Version.** This 4-bit field identifies the IP version number.
- **Traffic class.** This 8-bit field is similar in spirit to the TOS in IPv4.
- **Flow label.** This 20-bit field is used to identify a flow of datagrams.

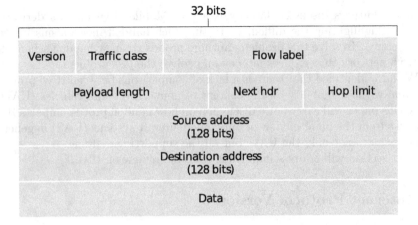

Fig. 1. IPv6 datagram. This figure was adapted from [12].

- **Payload length.** This 16-bit value is treated as an unsigned integer giving the number of bytes in the IPv6 datagram following the fixed-length, 40-byte datagram header.
- **Next header.** This field identifies the protocol to which the contents (data field) of this datagram will be delivered (for example, to TCP or UDP).
- **Hop limit.** The contents of this field are decremented by one by each router that forwards the datagram. If the hop limit count reaches zero, the datagram is discarded.
- **Source and destination addresses.** The various formats of the IPv6 128-bit address are described in RFC 4291 [8].
- **Data.** This is the payload portion of the IPv6 datagram. When the datagram reaches its destination, the payload will be removed from the IP datagram and passed on to the protocol specified in the next header field.

3.1 Mobile IPv6

Mobile IPv6 (MIPv6) describes the protocol operations needed to keep a mobile node connected to the Internet during its handover from one access router to another. These operations involve movement detection, IP address configuration, and location update (RFC 4068) [11]. Mobile IPv6 is an IETF standard that has added the roaming capabilities of mobile nodes in IPv6 network (RFC 3775) [10].

The major benefit of this standard is that the mobile nodes (as IPv6 nodes) change their point-of-attachment to the IPv6 Internet without changing their IP address [6]. Moreover, MIPv6 is an update to Mobile IP (RFC 6275) [18], designed to authenticate mobile devices using IPv6 addresses.

In traditional IP network routing, addresses represent a topology. The routing mechanisms were made under the assumption that each network node has always the same entry point to the Internet and that each IP address identifies the link to which it is connected. MIPv6 allows a mobile node to transparently maintain connections as it moves from a network edge to another.

4 HAMSTER Architecture

The Healthy, Mobility and Security-based Data Communication Architecture (HAMSTER) is divided into three main versions according to the most common types of unmanned vehicles (UV): aerial, ground and aquatic. Moreover, two special platforms are defined: the first one is intended to control security and safety aspects under all architecture versions, and the second one aims at mobility aspects and external communications. Figure 2 presents an overview of HAMSTER hierarchical organisation.

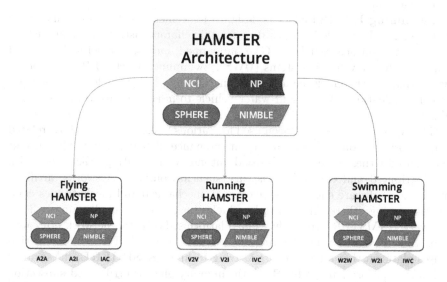

Fig. 2. HAMSTER versions and the specific modules for mobility (NIMBLE) and safety and security (SPHERE).

Flying HAMSTER deals exclusively with the aerial segment. It was defined based on specific characteristics and requirements of unmanned aerial vehicles (UAV) and unmanned aircraft systems (UAS). Flying HAMSTER deals specifically with internal airplane communication (IAC), airplane-to-airplane communication (A2A) and airplane-to-infrastructure communication (A2I).

The main applications of UAVs are related to agricultural and environmental monitoring, safety, military and civil defense. The aircraft is usually able to capture images for processing relevant information about a specific field, which may contribute to improve productivity. There are several cases where they might be applied in environmental and borders monitoring, or even applied as aerial sensors in networks for disaster management [20] and multiple UAV applications [3, 13, 14, 24, 28].

Running HAMSTER deals specifically with vehicles on terrestrial segment. It was defined based on specific characteristics and requirements of unmanned ground vehicles (UGV) and unmanned ground systems (UGS). Running HAMSTER treats internal vehicle communication (IVC), vehicle-to-vehicle communication (V2V) and vehicle-to-infrastructure communication (V2I).

The objective of ground vehicles may vary from driver support in possible dangerous situations with the intention of preventing road accidents, to autonomous driving with no human intervention, which could be used in urban traffic, agriculture, industry and safety applications [29]. The sensor fusion technique is used for integration of multiple sensors such as cameras, digital compasses, and GPS, allowing the vehicle to become autonomous in both urban and rural areas [25].

Swimming HAMSTER was designed for vehicles that operate on aquatic environments. It was defined based on specific characteristics and requirements of unmanned surface vehicles (UGV), unmanned undersea vehicles (UUV) and unmanned water vehicles systems (UWS). Swimming HAMSTER is composed by internal water vehicle communication (IWC), water vehicle-to-water vehicle communication (W2W) and water vehicle-to-infrastructure communication (W2I).

The aquatic vehicles have been used for various tasks, especially those related to monitoring of oil exploration and maintenance of hydropower. The current challenges for these vehicles go beyond autonomy, integrating other areas with the distributed and embedded systems, such as computer networks, artificial intelligence, software engineering, electrical, mechanical and mechatronics engineering, among others. The multiple vehicles tasks are also challenging [1, 30].

Every HAMSTER version has four platforms: **NCI**, the network criticality index that measures a node's criticality within a network; **NP**, the navigation phases platform that aims at energy saving techniques; **SPHERE**, the security and safety platform; and **NIMBLE**, the mobility platform [19]. Next subsection will briefly introduce NIMBLE, the HAMSTER's platform for mobility which is the focus of this paper.

4.1   NIMBLE: Mobility Platform

Be it an infrastructured network or a mobile ad hoc network, mobility is an important requirement for UVs. In the air, mobility can be even more challenging than in roads and in the ocean, but all of them have somehow a demand for mobility. Naturally, ad hoc is the most challenging operating mode, since it does not rely on a fixed centralised access point and nodes move at high speeds and (sometimes) in unpredicted paths. Although seeming not so challenging, infrastructure-based communications may demand mobility approaches as well. That way, NIMBLE was conceived with the view to encompass mobility in M2X communications on HAMSTER architecture. It stands for NatIve MoBiLity platform for unmanned systEms.

Communication is a crucial aspect of, and one of the biggest challenges in, the design of multiple-vehicle systems [3,5]. In the simplest scenario, all vehicles are directly connected to a common infrastructure, and this can act as an intermediary for all communications among them. However, this strategy has several problems. Firstly, each vehicle must be equipped with expensive and complex hardware in order to perform the long-distance communication with the control station or satellite. Secondly, many factors may compromise communication reliability such as changing environmental conditions, the high mobility of vehicles, different terrain topologies, or obstacles. Finally, the typical use of a ground control station (GCS) to provide the communication infrastructure limits the mission target locations to the GCS coverage area, since beyond that vehicles disconnect from the network, and become unreachable.

The implementation of an ad hoc network connecting all vehicles is one of the most feasible alternatives to infrastructure-based communication. An ad hoc network is composed by nodes that also act as routers, forming a temporary network with no fixed topology or centralised administration [23]. This approach increases the mission target area, since communications among vehicles and the GCS can be routed through other vehicles in a series of hops. Also, even if there is no connection to a GCS, the nodes can form an ad hoc network to share information or work in cooperation.

Ad hoc networks are classified according to their implementation, utilization, communication and mission objectives. If the nodes that compose an ad hoc network are mobile, the network is classified as MANET (Mobile Ad hoc NETwork). For vehicle-specific applications, MANETs are sub-divided into UANET (Underwater Ad hoc NETwork) for aquatic vehicles, VANET (Vehicular Ad hoc NETwork) for terrestrial vehicles, or FANET (Flying Ad hoc NETwork) for aerial vehicles [2,22], as illustrated by Fig. 3.

Each type of vehicular network faces different, unique challenges: for instance, a UANET must deal with an underwater transmission medium, and VANETs often encounter unexpected road obstacles. However, it has been recognized that FANETs have to address more challenging issues than other ad hoc networks [2,22], because of the following specific characteristics:

- **Higher node mobility.** FANET nodes typically have higher mobility than those in other types of MANET. As a result, a FANET's network topology can change more frequently, which increases the overhead caused by connecting and routing operations.
- **Multiple connections.** In many applications, the nodes in FANETs collect environmental data and then retransmit it to the control station, similarly to wireless sensor networks [21]. Therefore, FANETs have to manage multiple communications between UAVs and monitoring stations, as well as providing support to peer-to-peer connections among UAVs.
- **Very low node density.** Typical distances among nodes in FANETs are usually longer than in MANETs and VANETs clapper2007unmanned; thus, the communication range in FANETs must also be greater than in other

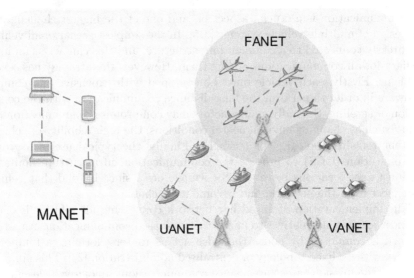

Fig. 3. Relationships between different types of mobile ad hoc networks (MANET): underwater ad hoc networks (UANET), vehicular ad hoc networks (VANET) and flying ad hoc networks (FANET).

networks. This imposes more demanding requirements for radio links and other hardware elements.
– **Heterogeneity.** UAV systems may include heterogeneous sensors, and each of them may require different strategies for data distribution.
– **Obstacles.** Due to the higher node mobility, obstacles may randomly block links among UAVs, which must be addressed in order to provide different temporary communication paths, avoiding the disconnection of nodes.

External communications on HAMSTER architeture are dealt by NIMBLE platform. Figure 4 illustrates NIMBLE's submodules: ADHOC and INFRA.

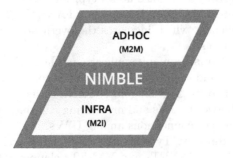

Fig. 4. NIMBLE mobility platform is composed by ADHOC and INFRA submodules for external communications.

M2M communications, including mostly MANET and derivative networks, are managed by ADHOC. On the other hand, INFRA is aimed at the management of infrastructured communications e.g. sattelites and GCS (in HAMSTER case, identified as CAGE). These submodules also concentrate efforts on mobility models improvements.

The separation into two different modules provides the avantage of allowing better approaches to each external communication. For instance, while communicating with an infrastructure, INFRA submodule will most certainly need to transmit with higher signal strength due to longer distances from the UV to the infrastructured element. On the contrary, while communicating with other UVs, ADHOC should use appropriate ad hoc routing protocols for better message delivery.

This paper tests specifically NIMBLE's INFRA handoff process focused on avionics. Next section presents the methodology.

5 Methodology

This section presents the simulator used for experiments execution, and the criteria and results collection methods.

5.1 OMNeT++

OMNeT++ is an extensible, modular, component-based C++ simulation library and framework, primarily for building network simulators [17]. Due to its general structure, it can be used for analysis and study of different problems, including:

1. Modelling wired/wireless communication networks;
2. Protocols;
3. Architecture validation and distributed systems modelling;
4. Performance evaluation of complex systems;
5. Modeling and simulation of any system in which the approach to discrete event is appropriate, and entities can be conveniently mapped.

OMNeT++ provides a component architecture for models. Components (modules) are programmed in C++, then assembled into larger components and models using a high-level language (NED). Reusability of models comes for free. OMNeT++ has extensive GUI support, and due to its modular architecture, the simulation kernel (and models) can be embedded easily into applications [17].

In addition to OMNeT++, this project uses INET [9]. INET Framework is an open-source model library for the OMNeT++ simulation environment. It provides protocols, agents and other models for researchers and students working with communication networks. INET is especially useful when designing and validating new protocols, or exploring new or exotic scenarios.

INET contains models for the Internet stack (TCP, UDP, IPv4, IPv6, OSPF, BGP, etc.), wired and wireless link layer protocols (Ethernet, PPP, IEEE 802.11, etc.), support for mobility, MANET protocols, DiffServ, MPLS with LDP and RSVP-TE signalling, several application models, and many other protocols and components. Several other simulation frameworks take INET as a base, and extend it into specific directions, such as vehicular networks, overlay/peer-to-peer networks, or LTE [9].

OMNeT++ simulator was chosen to run the simulations that will be discussed in Sect. 6. We have implemented two simulations using INET Framework and OMNeT++ to compare distinct handoff processes: with and without mobility.

Nest subsection provides details on criteria and results collection.

5.2   Criteria and Results Collection

First, we have investigated a way of making simulations as similar as possible. For instance, the speed at which the MU would move, plus routers distance and coverage area must be the same in both simulations, in order not to compromise results. Criteria used for comparison between algorithms are: process time and signal strength.

The handoff run time criterion is perhaps the most complex and that best defines the difference between processes. For some algorithms, it is highly important for a handoff process to be performed as fast as possible due to the fact that the MU needs to disconnect from previous AP to start sending requests to the next one. Packet losses may occur due to disconnected time [26]. For example, if there is a real-time video transmission, packets will likely be lost causing issues.

The handoff process can be divided into two phases [16], as shown in Fig. 5. For further analysis, the run time is measured for each step separately, allowing a step by step comparison. The first phase is defined as search. The MU scans for nearby available APs. Once found, the AP in better conditions according to the algorithm criteria, is the one chosen by MU for connection establishment.

Search phase can be divided into two steps: scanning delay and classification delay. Still, in scanning delay, it is possible to scan each channel separately. In practice, the initial event of the search phase is Beacon Timeout, i.e., the MU has received at least three Beacon packets that were considered as noise, representing a connection lost state, which leads to a new search for APs. In the next event, the MU disassociates from AP1 and sends an internal command to tune the channel 0, starting a new search. The scanning delay ends in the event when the MU radio can tune channel 0, and then start the effective search.

The next step consists on scanning each channel in order to find an AP. This scan takes place as follows: the MU tunes to a certain channel and listens for incoming messages from any AP in that frequence, should it be a Beacon or a Router Advertisement. Such listening process lasts a preset time. After that, the MU is aware whether there is any AP operating in that frequency that can be include on the list of new AP candidate. If a channel has been scanned and no

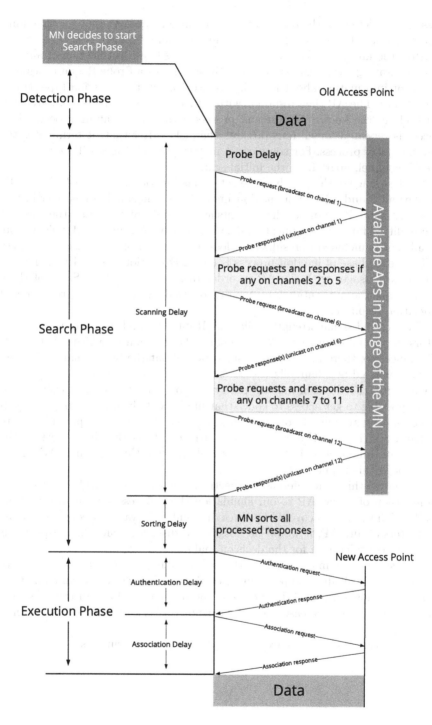

Fig. 5. Phases of handoff process. This figure was adapted from [16].

message was detected, the radio warns the management layer that the time limit is over and no AP was found. A command for channel change is also triggered.

After the minimum scanning time and the positive identification of another device operating on the same frequency, the MU sends a Probe Request message, asking for information about how the AP works, e.g. transmission type, transmission rate. The AP then responds with a Probe Response message. Later, the MU updates the known AP list and proceeds with the scanning process. This process is repeated for all four possible channels. After that, it terminates the scanning delay process. For comparison matters, search times will be measured on each channel, apart from the initial scan phase.

The last stage of the search phase is the classification delay, in which the MU classifies all found APs. A limitation imposed by our simulator is seen in this phase. Although it simulates these events as concomitant processes, they are not so in reality. Thus, the classification delay cannot be measured in details, but its overall time is included in results and does not imply problems for our analyses.

The next phase of handoff process is called Execution Phase. Here, the MU exchanges messages with the AP in order to associate with it. Some of these messages are the authentication request, followed by its response, request and association response.

The received signal strength indicator (RSSI) of an AP is one of the decisive factors of a handoff process. When making the decision of which AP the MU will connect to, there must be a consideration about the best signal, which can potentially avoid new handoffs.

Changing the decision-making policy can be a tricky task, since it is not always possible to get access to codes that implement the direct process in real-time operating systems. In our experiments, such change is not possible due to simulator restrictions. However, we will carry out tests that help checking the influence of some factors in the decision-making algorithm used by OMNeT++ simulator in this paper.

To analyse this by a different perspective, a new scenario has been proposed: the inclusion of a new AP to our simulation that addresses a scenario with no mobility. Thus, an area covered by three different APs was created. By changing parameters of any AP, it would be possible to discuss about which aspect was taken into consideration for the decision making.

The aspects we aim to analyse with this research are signal strength and data transfer rate. Basically, the positioning of all three routers forms an equilateral triangle, as shown in Fig. 6. In each test, the parameter of one of the APs were modified in order to decrease one of its features. Afterward, scenarios in Table 4 were proposed.

Next section presents the experimental setup for experiments.

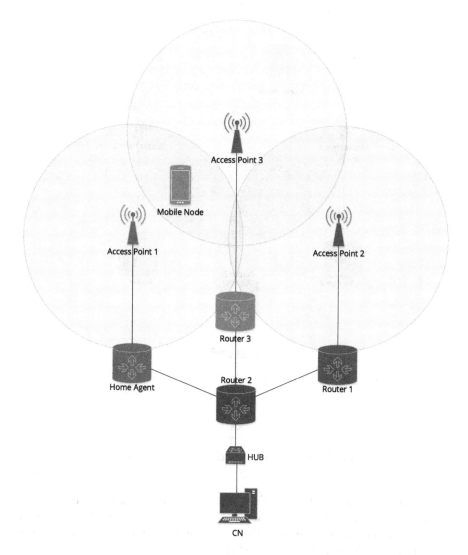

Fig. 6. Network scheme adopted for testing handoff decision making algorithm.

6   Experimental Setup

6.1   IPv6 with Mobility

The "IPv6 with Mobility" simulation (*MIPv6Network.ned*) is part of the INET simulations package [9]. This simulation allows the analysis of handoff process on an IPv6 network with mobility.

The MIPv6Network is composed by five basic elements: mobile unit, access points, routers, hub and fixed host. In addition, there are two elements in charge of configuration. Figure 7 illustrates the scenario.

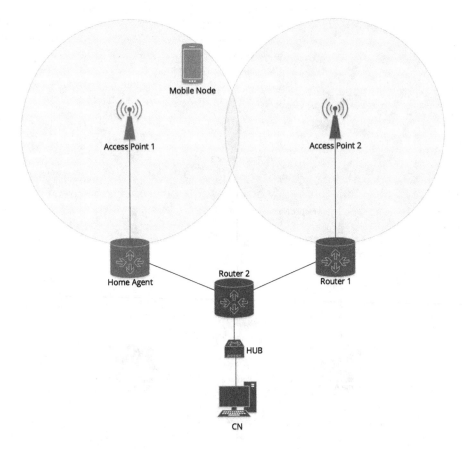

Fig. 7. Graphical representation of MIPv6Network.

The MU is composed by a *WirelessHost6* module. It is the MU, which is always connected to an AP and moves among coverage areas. The APs used in the simulation are both equal. They provide radio for routers i.e. wireless communication between MU and Fixed Host.

The first router module, identified as *Router6*, acts as Home Agent. This router captures packets for the MU should it be connected or not. The Router called *R_1* is the Foreign Agent, i.e. it distributes the packets generated by the MU while outside the original network, and acts receiving the tunnelled packets destined to MU. The other Router along with the Hub represents the Internet, providing the tunnel between Routers that provide connectivity.

6.2   IPv6 Without Mobility

We have developed the "IPv6 wihout Mobility" simulation (*handoff_ipv6.ned*) in order to meet the requirements we are investigating. This IPv6 network performs experiments of handoff without mobility. As the MU moves from one network to another, considering there is no support for mobility, it completely loses its link with the native address, including a subsequent IP address change.

Figure 8 illustrates the simulation. One can point out that the network is formed by a *WirelessHost6* MU that supports MIPv6, but it has such a feature disabled. As seen in "IPv6 with Mobility" simulation, two APs are used for wireless communication between routers. They are both independent routers that provide distinct links. This is a way of guaranteeing that no mobility is used in our experiments.

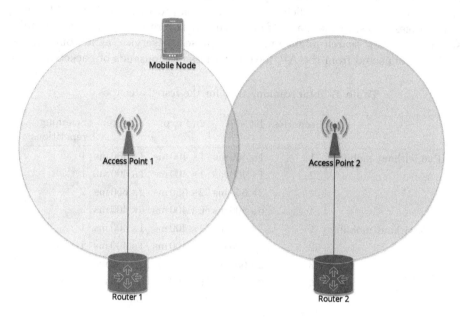

Fig. 8. Graphical representation of handoff_ipv6 network.

In addition to the network elements, two configuration modules were used: *ChannelControl* (for managing wireless communications, including distances and possible interferences), and *flatNetworkConfigurator6* (which manages addresses issues and routing tables).

Next section will present results and discussions.

7 Results and Discussions

7.1 Run Time Results

As mentioned in "Methodology" section, the time needed for a MU to either interpret three lost *Beacons* and decide to start a new search, cannot be calculated with our simulator. Thus, it will not be considered for comparison purposes, since it does not affect the results integrity.

Table 1 presents the measured run times of total scanning of frequency channels during handoff process in both simulations. The factor which was more decisive on run time was the number of scans that the MU had to perform before finding an available AP. This difference is noticeable in scenarios where there is intersection between the signal coverage areas (Scenarios 1 and 2) than those with no intersection (Scenarios 2 and 3). If there is no intersection, as the MU loses the first AP signal, it initiates a search on all channels. If this time is not enough for the MU to enter the area of another AP, it will have to perform other complete search. Repeating these searches is a very costly process that also compromises the efficiency of the handoff process, since each additional search takes 1.25 s. In a scenario of high transmission rates, e.g. in a video/audio streaming, a new search might fully compromise the service, as it would mean 1.25 s disconnected from the AP, meaning a loss of thousands of packets.

Table 1. Total scanning time for the tested scenarios.

	Scenarios	1st exp.	2nd exp.	3rd exp.	Scanning repetitions
IPv6 without mobility	1	1 s 400 ms	1 s 400 ms	1 s 400 ms	1
	2	1 s 400 ms	1 s 400 ms	1 s 400 ms	1
	3	2 s 650 ms	2 s 650 ms	2 s 650 ms	2
	4	6 s 400 ms	6 s 400 ms	6 s 400 ms	5
IPv6 without mobility	1	1 s 400 ms	1 s 400 ms	1 s 400 ms	1
	62	1 s 400 ms	1 s 400 ms	1 s 400 ms	1
	3	2 s 650 ms	2 s 650 ms	2 s 650 ms	2
	4	6 s 400 ms	6 s 400 ms	6 s 400 ms	3

Still, in Table 1, one can point out that the velocity of a mobile node directly impacts the handoff time on a situation in which there is no intersection of cells. As the MU moves faster through the area without signal, it needs to perform fewer scans and therefore connect faster to the new AP.

In the second phase of handoff process, it is performed authentication and association of the MU with the AP. The authentication delay times are shown in Table 2 and the association delay times are shown in Table 3.

The next handoff phase that impacts the total run time is the authentication/association process. In the case of authentication, there is a difference in microseconds among all tested scenarios. In both scenarios, the IPv6 protocol without mobility performed better than MIPv6 (Scenarios 2 and 3). On the other hand, MIPv6 performed better in the other two. In association phase, MIPv6 took advantage in three scenarios, not being the best option only in the case of travel speed and no cells intersection. This result indicates that MIPv6 can facilitate the MU association process.

Finally, Table 4 shows the total handoff process run time in all eight tested scenarios.

Table 2. Authentication delay times for the tested scenarios.

	Scenarios	1st exp.	2nd exp.	Mean time
IPv6 without mobility	1	2 ms 375 us 943 ns	2 ms 375 us 943 ns	2 ms 375 us 943 ns
	2	2 ms 376 us 59 us	2 ms 376 us 59 us	2 ms 376 us 59 us
	3	2 ms 376 us 188 us	2 ms 376 us 188 us	2ms 376 us 188 us
	4	2 ms 403 us 214 us	2 ms 403 us 214 us	2 ms 403 us 214 us
IPv6 without mobility	1	2 ms 349 us 88 us	2 ms 349 us 88 us	2 ms 349 us 88 us
	2	2 ms 403 us 226 us	2 ms 403 us 226 us	2 ms 403 us 226 us
	3	2 ms 402 us 582 us	2 ms 402 us 582 us	2ms 402 us 582 us
	4	2 ms 402 us 609 us	2 ms 402 us 609 us	2 ms 402 us 609 us

Table 3. Association delay times for the tested scenarios.

	Scenarios	1st exp.	2nd exp.	Mean time
IPv6 without mobility	1	1 ms 523 us 971 us	1 ms 523 us 971 us	1 ms 523 us 971 us
	2	1 ms 506 us 29 us	1 ms 506 us 29 us	1 ms 506 us 29 us
	3	1 ms 497 us 94 us	1 ms 497 us 94 us	1 ms 497 us 94 us
	4	1 ms 507 us 70 us	1 ms 507 us 70 us	1 ms 507 us 70 us
IPv6 without mobility	1	1 ms 479 us 44 us	1 ms 479 us 44 us	1 ms 479 us 44 us
	2	1 ms 497 us 113 us	1 ms 497 us 113 us	1 ms 497 us 113 us
	3	1 ms 496 us 805 us	1 ms 496 us 805 us	1 ms 496 us 805 us
	4	1 ms 523 us 387 us	1 ms 523 us 387 us	1 ms 523 us 387 us

One can observe in Table 4 the predominance of scan time if compared to authentication and association delays, which go from 300 times and reach up to 2000 times higher. It is important to point out that IPv6 without mobility performed better and faster in three scenarios.

As a final remark, a few microseconds (less than 100 µs in all cases) do not considerably affect the amount of received bits. For example, in a 2 Mbps

Table 4. Total handoff time for the tested scenarios.

	Scenarios	Total time
IPv6 without mobility	1	1 s 403 ms 899 us 971 us
	2	1 s 403 ms 882 us 88 us
	3	2 s 653 ms 873 us 282 us
	4	6 s 403 ms 910 us 278 us
IPv6 without mobility	1	1 s 403 ms 828 us 132 us
	2	1 s 403 ms 900 us 339 us
	3	2 s 653 ms 899 us 207 us
	4	6 s 403 ms 925 us 996 us

transmission, around 2 bits per millisecond (ms) are sent — or 0.002 bits per microsecond (μs). Differences of 100 μs result in the loss of 0.2 bit, which is extremely small considering the amount of transmitted information.

7.2   Decision Making

In the first scenario for decision making evaluation, both APs are configured to emit signals with the same power. However, AP1 operated with half the AP2's data transmission rate. At the end of scan, the handoff algorithm chose to connect to AP1, as shown in Fig. 9.

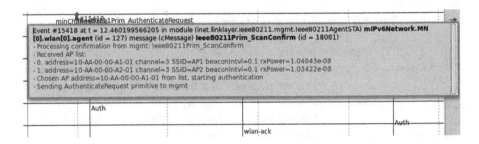

Fig. 9. Handoff classification phase on Scenario 1.

The other analysed scenario contains two APs with the same data transmission rate, however different signal strength. The algorithm has chosen to associate with AP1, as shown in Fig. 10.

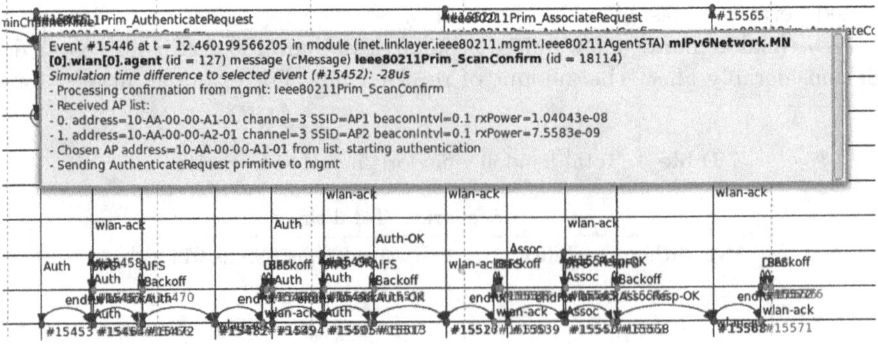

Fig. 10. Handoff classification phase on Scenario 2.

Regarding tests on Decision Making, the main conclusion is that the predominant factor in choosing an AP to connect was the signal strength received by MU at the scanning process. In the test performed in Scenario 1, in which both APs operate with equal signal strength, and AP1 operates with half the transfer rate of AP2, AP1 was chosen. This can be explained by the difficulty in obtaining an overall symmetry of the problem: as much as the APs are equally distributed, in the meantime while receiving the packet with information about each AP signal strength, the MU has already moved. That leads to slight differences in results, as shown in Fig. 9. The predominance of signal quality explains the choice for AP1, despite the low transmission rate.

The experiment in the second scenario only confirms the conclusion aforementioned. When signal strength was far different, the chosen AP was always the one that offered a higher signal quality.

It is important to clarify that tests conducted to observe decision making were carried out in only one of the protocols mentioned in this paper, the "IPv6 with Mobility". This choice was made due to the fact that the decision making algorithm is linked to the simulator itself, not to the protocols. Thus, for any handoff process in any OMNeT++ simulation, the decision making algorithm was the same. The purpose of these tests were to get more information about this algorithm and complement researches on handoff processes, and also to draw conclusions that could help UAVs development and research. Such a discussion will be presented in next section.

8   A Discussion on Safety-Critical Systems

As it could be seen in presented and discussed results, there is a small advantage of "IPv6 without Mobility" when compared to "IPv6 with Mobility", specifically regarding handoff run time. Considering real-time systems, although seeming irrelevant, such a small difference can be very important. In some applications, such as aviation, critical embedded systems must have low failure rates, such as a serious failure every 10^5 até 10^9 h of operation at most. Whereas delays in communication can lead to failures, this difference becomes significant.

Taking the example of scenarios where terrestrial or aquatic vehicles operate missions in isolated areas and UAVs are used to fly and collect/provide information for terrestrial and aquatic networks, the flyovers cannot be performed more than once depending on the local access conditions. In some cases, the UAV flight range limit is very short, requiring the flight to be performed with higher speed and only once. In this case, handoff process run time for connection among UAV and terrestrial/aquatic vehicles could significantly impact the overall system.

Another practical example is related to smart cars and roads. On highways with multiple APs, handoff operations happen frequently, which can lead to inherent delays that may affect both safety and entertainment operations. Thus, the mentioned small differences in run time can be important and should be taken into account on these systems design, especially for real-time applications.

9   Conclusions

This paper carried out a comparative evaluation between two IPv6 network based handoff processes, with and without mobility. Some parameters such as run time and decision making were taken into account for performance analysis. In fact, the simulated results presented a slight advantage of handoff process without mobility. As for real-time systems, such a small difference may be very representative.

Although tests were conducted in a completely deterministic simulation and the decision making algorithm was the same in both models, this paper presented results that help researchers and developers to have insights on embedded systems behaviour using IPv6 protocol facing different handoff situations. These experiments are part of the implementation of NIMBLE platform for mobility on unmanned vehicles.

As future work we aim to perform similar experiments in real embedded systems prototypes running real-time operating systems (RTOS). These operating systems meet the needs of such systems, and might also improve the communication performance. Moreover, new scenarios of UV applications should be taken as examples for new experiments.

References

1. Abbott-McCune, S., Kobezak, P., Tront, J., Marchany, R., Wicks, A.: UGV: security analysis of subsystem control network. In: Karlsen, R.E., Gage, D.W., Shoemaker, C.M., Gerhart, G.R. (eds.) Proceedings of SPIE - The International Society for Optical Engineering, Baltimore, MD, vol. 8741, p. 87410Z (2013). doi:10.1117/12.2016314
2. Bekmezci, I., Sahingoz, O.K., Temel, S.: Flying ad-hoc networks (FANETs): a survey. Ad Hoc Netw. **11**(3), 1254–1270 (2013). doi:10.1016/j.adhoc.2012.12.004
3. Bouachir, O., Abrassart, A., Garcia, F., Larrieu, N.: A mobility model for UAV ad hoc network. In: 2014 International Conference on Unmanned Aircraft Systems (ICUAS), pp. 383–388. IEEE (2014). doi:10.1109/ICUAS.2014.6842277
4. Chuang, M.C., Lee, J.F.: FH-PMIPv6: a fast handoff scheme in proxy mobile IPv6 networks. In: 2011 International Conference on Consumer Electronics, Communications and Networks (CECNet), pp. 1297–1300. IEEE (2011). doi:10.1109/CECNET.2011.5768193
5. Chung, H., Oh, S., Shim, D.H., Sastry, S.S.: Toward robotic sensor webs: algorithms, systems, and experiments. Proc. IEEE **99**(9), 1562–1586 (2011). doi:10.1109/JPROC.2011.2158598
6. Das, K.: Mobile IPv6: What is Mobile IPv6? (2017). http://ipv6.com/articles/mobile/Mobile-IPv6.htm
7. Gupta, L., Jain, R., Vaszkun, G.: Survey of important issues in UAV communication networks. IEEE Commun. Surv. Tutor. **18**(2), 1123–1152 (2016). doi:10.1109/COMST.2015.2495297
8. Hinden, R., Deering, S.: RFC 4291 - IP version 6 addressing architecture. Technical report, IETF Tools (2006). https://tools.ietf.org/html/rfc4291.html
9. INET: Network MIPv6 Documentation (2017). https://github.com/inet-framework/inet/blob/master/examples/mobileipv6/MIPv6Network.ned

10. Johnson, D., Perkins, C., Arkko, J.: RFC 3775 - mobility support in IPv6. Technical report, IETF Tools (2004). https://www.ietf.org/rfc/rfc3775.txt
11. Koodli, R.: RFC 4068 - fast handovers for mobile IPv6. Technical report, IETF Tools (2005). https://tools.ietf.org/html/rfc4068
12. Kurose, J.F., Ross, K.W.: Computer Networking: A Top-Down Approach, 5th edn. Addison Wesley, Boston (2009)
13. Luo, C., Ward, P., Cameron, S., Parr, G., McClean, S.: Communication provision for a team of remotely searching UAVs: a mobile relay approach. In: 2012 IEEE Globecom Workshops, pp. 1544–1549. IEEE (2012). doi:10.1109/GLOCOMW.2012.6477815
14. Maza, I., Caballero, F., Capitán, J., Martínez-de Dios, J.R., Ollero, A.: Experimental results in multi-UAV coordination for disaster management and civil security applications. J. Intell. Robot. Syst. **61**(1–4), 563–585 (2011). doi:10.1007/s10846-010-9497-5
15. Mishra, A., Shin, M., Arbaugh, W.: An empirical analysis of the IEEE 802.11 MAC layer handoff process. ACM SIGCOMM Comput. Commun. Rev. **33**(2), 93 (2003). doi:10.1145/956981.956990
16. Nankani, A.: Horizontal handoffs within WLANs. Ph.D. thesis, Master thesis, Department of Microelectronics and Information Technology, Royal Institute of Technology (KTH) Sweden (2005). ftp://ftp.it.kth.se/Reports/DEGREE-PROJECT-REPORTS/28
17. OMNeT++ Discrete Event Simulator: What is OMNeT++? (2017). https://omnetpp.org/intro
18. Perkins, C., Johnson, D., Arkko, J.: RFC 6275 - mobility support in IPv6. Technical report, IETF Tools (2011). https://tools.ietf.org/html/rfc6275
19. Pigatto, D.F., Gonçalves, L., Roberto, G.F., Rodrigues Filho, J.F., Floro da Silva, N.B., Pinto, A.R., Lucas Jaquie Castelo Branco, K.R.: The HAMSTER data communication architecture for unmanned aerial, ground and aquatic systems. J. Intell. Robot. Syst. 1–19 (2016). doi:10.1007/s10846-016-0356-x
20. Quaritsch, M., Kruggl, K., Wischounig-Strucl, D., Bhattacharya, S., Shah, M., Rinner, B.: Networked UAVs as aerial sensor network for disaster management applications. Elektrotech. Informationstechnik **127**(3), 56–63 (2010). doi:10.1007/s00502-010-0717-2
21. Rieke, M., Foerster, T., Broering, A.: Unmanned aerial vehicles as mobile multi-sensor platforms. In: The 14th AGILE International Conference on Geographic Information Science, 18–21 April 2011, Utrecht, Netherlands (2011)
22. Sahingoz, O.K.: Networking models in flying ad-hoc networks (FANETs): concepts and challenges. J. Intell. Robot. Syst. **74**(1–2), 513–527 (2014). doi:10.1007/s10846-013-9959-7
23. Sarkar, S.K., Basavaraju, T.G., Puttamadappa, C.: Ad Hoc Mobile Wireless Networks: Principles, Protocols and Applications, 1st edn. Auerbach Publications, Boca Raton (2008)
24. Kim, S.-W., Seo, S.-W.: Cooperative unmanned autonomous vehicle control for spatially secure group communications. IEEE J. Sel. Areas Commun. **30**(5), 870–882 (2012). doi:10.1109/JSAC.2012.120604
25. Sun, Z., Wang, P., Vuran, M.C., Al-Rodhaan, M.A., Al-Dhelaan, A.M., Akyildiz, I.F.: BorderSense: border patrol through advanced wireless sensor networks. Ad Hoc Netw. **9**(3), 468–477 (2011). doi:10.1016/j.adhoc.2010.09.008
26. Tanenbaum, A.S., Wetherall, D.: Computer Networks. Pearson Prentice Hall, Upper Saddle River (2011)

27. Vatn, J.O.: An experimental study of IEEE 802.11 b handover performance and its effect on voice traffic. Technical report, Citeseer (2003)
28. Verma, A., Fernandes, R.: Persistent unmanned airborne network support for cooperative sensors. In: Proceedings of SPIE - The International Society for Optical Engineering, Baltimore, MD, vol. 8756, p. 87560J (2013). doi:10.1117/12.2018293
29. Wong, J.Y.: Theory of Ground Vehicles. Wiley, Hoboken (2008)
30. Xiang, X., Liu, C., Lapierre, L., Jouvencel, B.: Synchronized path following control of multiple homogenous underactuated AUVs. J. Syst. Sci. Complex. **25**(1), 71–89 (2012). doi:10.1007/s11424-012-0109-2

Recovery Effect in Low-Power Nodes of Wireless Sensor Networks

Leonardo M. Rodrigues[1]($\boxtimes$), Carlos Montez[1], Francisco Vasques[2], and Paulo Portugal[2]

[1] Federal University of Santa Catarina, Florianópolis, SC, Brazil
`l.m.rodrigues@posgrad.ufsc.br, carlos.montez@ufsc.br`
[2] Faculty of Engineering, University of Porto, Porto, Portugal
`{vasques,pportugal}@fe.up.pt`

Abstract. Energy consumption is a major concern in Wireless Sensor Networks (WSNs) since nodes are powered by batteries. Usually, batteries have low capacity and can not be replaced due to economic and/or logistical issues. In addition, batteries are complex devices as they depend on electrochemical reactions to generate energy. As a result, batteries exhibit non-linear behaviour over time, which makes difficult to estimate their lifetime. Analytical battery models are abstractions that allow estimating the battery lifetime through mathematical equations, taking into account important effects such as rate capacity and charge recovery. The recovery effect is very important since it enables charge gains in the battery after its electrochemical stabilization. Sleep scheduling approaches may take advantage of the recovery effect by adding sleep periods in the node activities in order to extend the network lifetime. This work aims to analyse the recovery effect within WSN context, particularly regarding low-power nodes. To do so, we use an analytical battery model for analysing the battery performance over time, during the node execution.

Keywords: WSN · Battery model · Recovery effect

1 Introduction

Wireless Sensor Networks (WSNs) are commonly composed of a large number of nodes, deployed in an area of interest, with self-management capacity [1]. Their nodes are characterized to be devices with processing, communication, and sensing capacities. Due to the reduction in manufacturing cost of the electronic components such as microcontrollers, transceivers, and sensors, WSNs are increasingly being adopted in many important application domains, including residential, commercial and industrial ones.

However, the nodes are usually powered by batteries and it is not feasible to replace the batteries of a large number of nodes for two reasons: cost and accessibility, mainly assuming that the deployments may occur in places with difficult access or which impose health risk. Thus, one of the great challenges of

© Springer International Publishing AG 2017
K. Branco et al. (Eds.): WoCCES 2013-2016, CCIS 702, pp. 45–62, 2017.
DOI: 10.1007/978-3-319-61403-8_3

WSNs lies in the power management of the nodes in order to save the energy consumption of the network as a whole.

Another factor that hinders the power management in WSN is related to the complexity of the batteries. In these components, electrochemical reactions are responsible for ensuring the power supply to the node. However, several factors (e.g., the discharge current intensity, operating temperature and chemical composition) may affect the battery operation. In this sense, it is common to observe a non-linear behaviour in these components over time.

In general, battery models aim to estimate the battery behaviour over time, which may include the knowledge about its lifetime, voltage level or State of Charge (SoC), for instance. Specifically, the analytical battery models are based on mathematical equations that consider the application load profile for estimating the battery lifetime. It is important that such models adequately represent the main effects that affect the batteries, such as the rate capacity and charge recovery, since the battery lifetime can be different if these effects are not considered during its use. Particularly, the recovery effect allows the battery to recompose part of its charge after reaching its internal electrochemical stability. In this context, it is important to insert periods of low-power consumption during the battery operation.

Sleep scheduling policies aim to switch nodes during the WSN activities to maximize their lifetime [2,3]. The sleep scheduling is an approach that takes advantage of the recovery effect by putting the nodes in low-power mode (or sleep mode) to save the network power as a whole. However, many studies perform simulations using sleep scheduling policies without considering both rate capacity and charge recovery effects, i.e., it is assumed that the batteries have a linear behaviour over time. This kind of assumption can affect the results of the simulations since batteries have much more complex behaviours, which are difficult to model.

This paper aims to conduct a study on the recovery effect in WSN nodes with low power characteristics. The assessments involve the use of an analytical battery model known as Kinetic Battery Model (KiBaM), which considers both rate capacity and charge recovery effects. These characteristics are important to minimize the error regarding the non-linear behaviour of the battery over time, mainly in WSN simulators. The main contributions of this work are as follows:

- Use of an analytical battery model within WSN context to assess the recovery effect in low-power consumption nodes.
- An analysis of several relevant scenarios to the WSN context, including assessments regarding recovery speed and the execution order of the tasks using the aforementioned KiBaM model.
- Results indicating the importance of the addition of low-power consumption periods during node activities to maximize its lifetime.

This paper is organized as follows. Section 2 presents the related work. Section 3 presents the concepts used in this work, including the battery basics and analytical battery models. Section 4 shows the set-up used in the simulations.

Section 5 presents the results for different scenarios considering the recovery effect on batteries. Section 6 concludes the paper and presents future work.

2   Related Work

There are many studies evaluating the use of battery models for application in mobile devices. Some of them focus in the context of WSN. This section presents an overview of the main analytical battery models in the literature, including some papers that compare the performance of such models and their application.

Manwell and McGowan [4,5] developed a battery model, based on the approach of chemical kinetics of Lead-Acid batteries, for use in time series performance models of hybrid energy systems. Such model requires the determination of three constants, unlike other existing models that typically require several constants to properly model the battery behaviour. Besides, the Kinetic Battery Model considers the rate capacity and charge recovery effects. The simulation results were compared with the BEST model (Battery Energy Storage Test).

Rakhmatov and Vrudhula [6,7] proposed a high-level battery model to help system designers to make battery-aware decisions. This model offers the ability to estimate the battery lifetime under a specific discharge current. Furthermore, it allows the trade-off between the estimation accuracy and the number of operations performed. Authors evaluate the results of the simulations based on a low-level simulator, known as DUALFOIL, which was set for Lithium-ion batteries. The results showed an average error of 3% in the predictions.

Rong and Pedram [8] presented a high-level analytical battery model to predict the remaining capacity of a Lithium-ion battery. However, this model needs to measure the battery output voltage and its temperature in an on-line way, which, according to the authors, can be obtained through the "smart battery" technology. The temperature and battery cycle aging effects are also considered in the model. Thus, it is possible to estimate the remaining capacity of the battery under different load conditions. Authors compare the results of predictions with simulations using DUALFOIL, reaching a maximum error of 5%.

Jongerden and Haverkort [9] indicate analytical battery models as the best type of model in the setting of performance modelling. In this context, authors performed a study on two well-known battery models: KiBaM and diffusion model. Some theoretical and practical comparisons were assessed in addition to demonstrating that the KiBaM is a first order approximation of the diffusion model. Finally, authors indicate the best battery model to use.

Chau et al. [10] examined the gain in the lifetime of Ni-MH batteries due to recovery effect. For this, the authors conducted several experiments with commercially available nodes (TelosB and Imote2). The paper shows that there is a substantial gain to utilize the benefits of the recovery effect, and indicate a threshold in which the charge recovery becomes insignificant. Based on that, it is proposed an energy-efficient duty cycle scheme which adjusts the duration of the transceiver sleep period according to the recovery saturation in the battery.

Rohner et al. [11] investigated the use of battery models within WSN context, which means assess such models with respect to low duty cycles and short duration loads. The investigation includes the following models: Electrochemical (using BatteryDesignStudio), KiBaM and a Hybrid Model combining KiBaM with an electric circuit abstraction. The parameters used in all models were based on Lithium batteries (CR2032). The results using the electrochemical model presented high computational complexity, which increases the simulation runtime to impractical values ($\approx$50 days). Although KiBaM deals with the rate capacity and recovery effects, it showed little difference regarding the battery lifetime for the used load profiles. The hybrid model requires a series of experiments to determine its constants, in addition to the simulation time close to 1 h for the used load profiles. Finally, authors indicate a depth study of battery models with regard to their sensitivity and temporal aspects within WSN context.

Daniil et al. [12] compared the performance of three battery models for Lithium polymer batteries: Circuit-Based Model, Diffusion Model, and KiBaM. The authors' goal was to find the appropriate model for real-time applications. In addition to the precision, the study assesses the execution time on a specific hardware platform. The results showed greater accuracy when using the circuit-based model, however, it requires the use of constant RC elements to avoid increasing the execution times of the simulations. The diffusion model and KiBaM showed less accurate results. Nevertheless, the study indicates the use of KiBaM since it presents lower execution times in the simulations.

Rodrigues et al. [13] proposed the analytical Temperature-Dependent Kinetic Battery Model (T-KiBaM), which allows modelling the behaviour of batteries under different operating temperatures. Such a model is capable of handling both the charge and the voltage level for different battery technologies. The authors performed several experiments with Ni-MH batteries at different operating temperatures. Although performing evaluations only with constant discharge currents, the results show that the T-KiBaM model is more accurate than both the original KiBaM model and Peukert's Law, when considering different operating temperatures of the battery.

Analytical battery models are preferred for two main reasons: (i) flexibility in allowing the parameter adjustment for different battery technologies; and (ii) computational efficiency allowing simulations with execution times on the order of seconds or minutes. Other works apply the KiBaM to model the battery behaviour in mobile devices, such as smartphones [14,15] or Internet-of-Things systems [16].

This article proposes the use of the KiBaM to model the battery behaviour of low-power nodes within WSN context. The major focus is on the recovery effect assessment in situations commonly encountered in WSN applications, such as with nodes with long sleep periods (sleep scheduling schemes) or nodes operating with duty cycles, alternating periods of activity and inactivity.

3   Background

This section presents the key concepts involved in this paper. A brief explanation of the mode of operation and characteristics of the batteries is addressed. Then, some analytical battery models are presented.

3.1   Battery Basics

Batteries are essential to make the concept of mobility a reality. Basically, batteries are devices that contain one or more electrochemical cells capable of transforming chemical energy into electrical energy. The cells are formed by two terminals (electrodes): the positive (or cathode); and the negative (or anode). An electrolyte allows the flow of ions between the battery terminals [17].

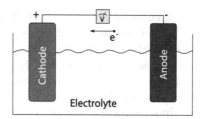

Fig. 1. Schematic of an electrochemical cell.

Generally, when discharging a battery, oxidation occurs at the anode, producing electrons (which flow through the external circuit) and positively charged ions (which, by diffusion, move through the electrolyte towards the cathode). Reduction reactions occur at the cathode, generating negatively charged ions. Figure 1 depicts the operation of a single cell battery.

There are primary and secondary batteries. *Primary batteries* can not be recharged, i.e., they do not support the reverse process of transforming electrical energy into chemical energy. Generally, this type of battery has a high specific energy, low cost, and long storage periods. *Secondary batteries* can be recharged by applying an electric current. Despite having higher initial cost, secondary batteries have a long life cycle and can be used several times before being discarded. Besides, they can withstand higher discharge currents.

There are three characteristics that define any secondary battery:

- Technology: relates the components interacting in the battery chemical reactions, the most common are Lead, Nickel, and Lithium. Batteries have different characteristics depending on the technology, being chosen according to the application requirements.
- Voltage: the open circuit voltage (V_{OC}) indicates the potential difference between the terminals of an electrochemical cell. The cut-off voltage (V_{cut}) indicates when a battery is no longer capable of withstanding the applied discharge current. This value is often used to indicate an "empty" battery.
- Capacity: normally in ampere-hours (Ah), it is the amount of available charge when the battery is discharged at a certain discharge current. The total capacity of a battery can be calculated by multiplying the discharge current applied by the time to reach V_{cut}.

Modelling the behaviour of batteries is a complex task since their characteristics depend on many factors such as the used technology, the operating temperature, the "age" of the cell etc. Thus, batteries have a non-linear behaviour. In this context, some battery models stand out for providing realistic estimates regarding the behaviour of the batteries over time. Some of these models are discussed in the following section.

3.2 Battery Models

This section presents the most common analytical battery models. These models describe the battery in an abstract way by modelling its properties through some equations [18]. The analytical battery models are computationally flexible since they involve the evaluation of analytical expressions [19].

Battery models help understand the battery behaviour over time according to the application requirements, without the need to conduct experiments with real WSN nodes. In this sense, adjustments in the node load profile can be performed to avoid the inefficient use of the available charge, which leads to the node failure and impairs the WSN coverage. Thus, each node maximizes its lifetime, being able to contribute to the network for the longest period possible.

There are several types of battery models: electrochemical, circuit-based, analytical, stochastic and hybrid. This work focuses on analytical battery models since they perform the prediction of the behaviour of batteries using equations that require few constants. This allows modelling different battery technologies with reduced effort. Some analytical battery models are shown below.

Peukert's Law is one of the simplest models for estimating the battery lifetime. This model considers only a part of the non-linear effects, relating the battery lifetime and the discharge rate. According to the Peukert's Law, the battery lifetime (L) can be approximated according to the following expression:

$$L = \frac{a}{I^b}, \tag{1}$$

where: I is the discharge current; a and b are constants dependent on the battery type, being obtained through experiments. However, the recovery effect is not part of this model. Thus, the results obtained with the Peukert's Law are considered good only for constant continuous loads, being inadequate when variable or intermittent loads are used [18].

Diffusion Model was introduced by Rakhmatov and Vrudhula [7]. This model describes the diffusion process of the active material in a battery. For example, it allows to estimate the battery lifetime (L), with a good approximation, for a given constant discharge current using the first ten terms of an infinite sum according to the following expression:

$$\alpha = 2I\sqrt{L} \left[1 + 2 \sum_{m=1}^{10} \left(e^{-\frac{\beta^2 m^2}{L}} - \frac{\pi e^{-\frac{\beta^2 m^2}{L}}}{\pi - 1 + \sqrt{1 + \pi \frac{L}{\beta^2 m^2}}} \right) \right], \tag{2}$$

where: α is the battery capacity; β captures the non-linear behaviour of the battery. Both parameters can be estimated through experimental data. However, as pointed out by Jongerden and Haverkort [18], the second-order differential equation makes it difficult to combine the model with a performance model.

Kinetic Battery Model (KiBaM) is an analytical battery model developed by Manwell and McGowan [4,5,20] that originally aims to model the behaviour of high-capacity Lead-Acid batteries. It uses an intuitive approach based on a two tank analogy to describe the charge/discharge processes. Figure 2 depicts the abstraction used in the model, including its constants.

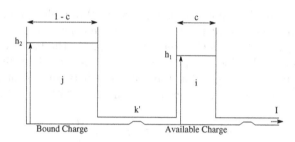

Fig. 2. Kinetic Battery Model (KiBaM) [4].

The *Available Charge* tank holds an electrical charge that can be immediately used for a device draining a current I. The *Bound Charge* tank holds a bounded charge that can flow towards the Available Charge tank, regulated by a valve with a fixed conductance k'. Such constant corresponds to the rate of a chemical diffusion/reaction process. Constant c corresponds to the total charge fraction stored in the Available Charge tank. A battery is exhausted when its Available Charge tank becomes empty, even if there is still charge in the Bound Charge tank. The transfer of charge, as well as the amount of unavailable charge, is proportional to the height difference between the two tanks, $\delta = (h_2 - h_1)$. Thus, a smaller difference between these two heights provides a longer lifetime for the battery [17]. The following system of differential equations describes the model.

$$\begin{cases} \frac{di}{dt} = -I + k'(h_2 - h_1) \\ \frac{dj}{dt} = -k'(h_2 - h_1), \end{cases} \tag{3}$$

where: i is the available charge and j is the bounded charge. The height values are calculated as $h_1 = i/c$ and $h_2 = j/(1-c)$, respectively. A new rate constant k is defined as:

$$k = \frac{k'}{c(1-c)}. \tag{4}$$

Replacing h_1, h_2 e k' in the system of differential Eq. (3), it results on:

$$\begin{cases} \frac{di}{dt} = -I - k(1-c)i + kcj \\ \frac{dj}{dt} = +k(1-c)i - kcj. \end{cases} \quad (5)$$

Laplace transforms are able to solve the system of differential equations [4], which results on:

$$\begin{cases} i = i_0 e^{-kt} + \frac{(y_0 kc - I)(1 - e^{-kt})}{k} - \frac{Ic(kt - 1 + e^{-kt})}{k} \\ j = j_0 e^{-kt} + y_0(1-c)(1 - e^{-kt}) - \frac{I(1-c)(kt - 1 + e^{-kt})}{k}, \end{cases} \quad (6)$$

where: i_0 and j_0 are the amount of charge in the Available Charge and Bound Charge tanks, respectively, at the beginning of the calculation ($t = 0$). In addition, $y_0 = i_0 + j_0$, where y_0 is the amount of charge in the battery at $t = 0$.

In the KiBaM model, the unavailable charge (u) is the height difference times $(1 - c)$ [17]. Equation (7) describes the difference between heights, denoted by δ, which is used to compute the unavailable charge (u) [21].

$$\delta = (h_2 - h_1) = \frac{j}{(1-c)} - \frac{i}{c} \quad (7)$$

$$u = (1-c) \cdot \delta \quad (8)$$

The reasoning behind δ value is important in order to obtain the battery nonlinear capacity variation [22]. Thus, KiBaM can model two important effects:

- *Rate Capacity* refers to the applied discharge current. The larger the load I, the faster the battery discharge and, thus, the lower its lifetime. This is due to the battery voltage level, which decays slowly during the battery discharge, reducing the effective capacity for high discharge currents [18];
- *Charge Recovery* refers to the ability of a battery to partially recover its charge during an idle period, after performing a discharge current I. This is due to the electrochemical stabilization inside the battery pack.

The non-linear battery behaviour arises, particularly, when these two effects act together. That is the case of WSN nodes operating in duty cycle schemes, i.e., periods during which the radio is in normal operation (high discharge currents), and periods during which it is in low power mode or sleep mode (low discharge currents). Figure 3 depicts an example with the behaviour over time in both tanks. In the fast discharge curve, the computing tasks consume: 250 mA (900 s), 100 µA (900 s) and 50 mA (2700 s). In the slow discharge curve, the computing tasks consume: 50 mA (900 s), 100 µA (900 s) and 5 mA (2700 s). Here, the parameters are adjusted to model a commercially available Ni-MH battery, as described by Manwell and McGowan [4], leading to $c = 0.828164$, $k = 0.021139$ s^{-1} and $y_0 = 2700$ As (≈ 750 mAh).

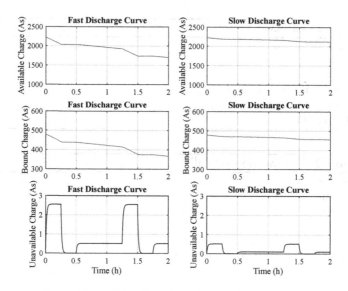

Fig. 3. An example of KiBaM behaviour over time.

4   Assessment Set-Up

This section describes the set-up used in the analysed scenarios. The simulations are performed in the Matlab[1], a scientific software for numerical computations. This choice is justified mainly by the following reasons: (i) easy implementation of mathematical models, (ii) ability to conduct simulations quickly using a multi-core computer, and (iii) ability to represent the results through custom graphics. Thus, we present the KiBaM function, implemented to perform the simulations, as well as the set of tasks used in the simulations. A study on the impact of different values for the KiBaM constants is also presented.

4.1   KiBaM Implementation

This section presents the KiBaM implementation in the function format, which is used in the assessments regarding the battery lifetime estimation on Matlab.

The KiBaM implementation can be summarized as a loop that performs function calls that drain the battery capacity, accounting for the time required to exhaust all its charge. Thus, it becomes possible to obtain the battery estimated lifetime in accordance with the applied discharge current and its respective execution time. Algorithm 1 shows how to implement the KiBaM function.

Lines 3 and 4 are responsible for updating the amount of charge in the Available Charge and Bound Charge tanks, respectively, according to Eq. (6). An example of the KiBaM function call is presented in Algorithm 2.

---

[1] http://www.mathworks.com/products/matlab/.

Algorithm 1. KiBaM function.

Data: c, k, i_0, j_0, t_0, I, t_I

1 $y_0 = i_0 + j_0$;
2 $t_0 = t_0 + t_I$;
3 $i_0 = \text{compute-i}(c, k, y_0, i_0, j_0, I, t_I)$;
4 $j_0 = \text{compute-j}(c, k, y_0, i_0, j_0, I, t_I)$;
5 **return** (i_0, j_0, t_0);

Algorithm 2. KiBaM function call.

Data: c, k, y_0, I, t_I

1 $i_0 = (c) * y_0$;
2 $j_0 = (1 - c) * y_0$;
3 $t_0 = 0$;
4 **while** $i_0 > 0$ **do**
5 $\quad|\quad [i_0, j_0, t_0] = \text{KiBaM}(c, k, i_0, j_0, t_0, I, t_I)$;
6 **end**
7 **print** (i_0, j_0, t_0);

The parameters that need an initial value are c, k and y_0 (the initial battery capacity), I (the discharge current) and t_I (the execution time of I). Throughout the execution, it becomes necessary to observe the amount of charge in the Available Charge tank, which can not be less than or equal to zero. Line 4 of the Algorithm 2 performs this verification.

4.2 Task Set

This section presents the tasks used in the assessment. In this case, a task consists of a node state and its respective execution time. Here, the tasks have the same power consumption of the Mica2 node, as described by Mikhaylov and Tervonen [23]. Table 1 shows the power consumption in each of the node states as well as its execution times, according to the simulated application.

For easy understanding, the tasks are named as follows: Tx (MCU+Tx), Rx (MCU+Rx), Ac (MCU-Active), and NS (Node-Standby). The first task, Tx, consumes 25.4 mA with an execution time of 4 min, representing the microcon-

Table 1. Discharge currents in a Mica2 node [23].

Short name	State	Discharge current (mA)	Execution time (min)
Tx	MCU+Tx	25.400	4
Rx	MCU+Rx	15.100	10
Ac	MCU-Active	8.000	6
NS	Node-Standby	0.019	0–20

troller (MCU) activity and the use of the transceiver to transmit data (Tx). The Rx task consumes 15.1 mA with an execution time equal to 10 min, representing the MCU activity and the use of the transceiver to receive data (Rx). The Ac task consumes 8 mA and has 6 min of execution time, representing only the MCU activity (transceiver off). Lastly, the NS task consumes 19 µA with execution times ranging between 0–20 min, according to the simulated scenario. This task represents the period in low-power mode (or sleep mode). Such task set is equivalent to an environmental monitoring application.

4.3   Comparison Between Different Values of k

This section presents a study regarding the use of different battery technologies (e.g., Lead-Acid, Ni-MH, Li-ion), which implies in different values for the KiBaM constants since the electrochemical characteristics of these technologies are distinct. This may change the recovery effect behaviour, so that the battery technology can be chosen according to the application requirements (e.g., discharge current, duty cycle and battery capacity).

The constant k is a time-dependent value. Thus, its value becomes critical to determine the time needed to transpose the charge from the Bound Charge tank to Available Charge tank, until the equilibrium in both tanks is reached. From the equilibrium point, it becomes unnecessary to maintain a low-power state, since there is no significant charge recovery. In this case, the time to reach the equilibrium point (stability) is called threshold.

In the simulations performed in this study, the values of c and y_0 are set in 0.625 and 2700 As [21], respectively. The values for the constant k are as follows: 0.05, 0.01, 0.005, 0.001, 0.0005 and 0.0001 s^{-1}. Besides, the following task sequence is performed: an MCU+TX state followed by a Node-standby state (with an 8-min execution time). This means a 33.33% duty cycle, i.e., the period in sleep mode is twice the period in active mode. Figure 4 depicts the simulation results with different values for the k constant.

Note that the behaviour of the discharge curves are different depending on the value of the k constant. In this case, the larger the value of k, the faster the charge transposition between the tanks and, thus, the shorter the time to reach the threshold. On the other hand, the lower the k value, the slower the charge transposition between the tanks. Consequently, the greater the time required to reach the threshold. Besides the difference in the recovery effect, there is a noticeable difference in battery lifetime. Table 2 shows the battery lifetime according to the value of k.

For this application, the most appropriate k value is 0.01 s^{-1} since it represents the best fit for a full charge recovery, i.e., without wasting time. This example highlights the importance of choosing the battery parameters that has characteristics similar to those used in the batteries in the real application.

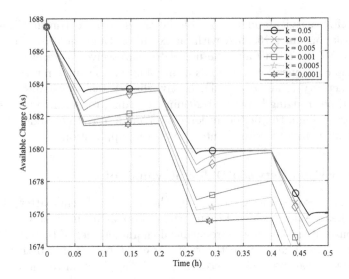

Fig. 4. Simulation with different k values.

Table 2. Difference in battery lifetime according to the k value.

k (s^{-1})	Battery lifetime (s)	Battery lifetime (h)
0.0500	318289	88.4136
0.0100	318280	88.4111
0.0050	317738	88.2606
0.0010	317622	88.2283
0.0005	316933	88.0369
0.0001	311951	86.6531

5   Assessment Results

This section aims to present the assessment results from different scenarios, focusing on the analysis of the charge recovery effect on batteries. Briefly, the recovery effect speed is analysed for the simulated application, as well as the influence of changing the sleep period order among the performed tasks. The execution order between tasks is also analysed. Finally, a case study regarding the frequency of switching between tasks is presented. The settings shown in Sect. 4 are used in these simulations, including the values of the KiBaM constants $(y_0, c$ and $k)$.

5.1   Recovery Effect: Speed Evaluation

This section shows how to properly choose the sleep period according to the application characteristics. In this sense, a comparison between different recovery times is performed. The goal is to choose an optimized sleep period for the set of tasks used so that recovery effect occurs without wasting time after reaching the threshold. Other details are presented below.

In this experiment, the task execution order is as follows: Tx, Rx, Ac, and NS. The execution times of the tasks are the same as shown in Table 1. In this case, the adopted periods for the Node-Standby task are 5, 10, 15 and 20 min. Such periods represent duty cycles of 20%, 33.33%, 42.85% and 50%, respectively. All simulated experiments are performed cyclically until the content in the Available Charge tank reach the minimum level. Figure 5(a) depicts the behaviour of the simulations when these tasks are used.

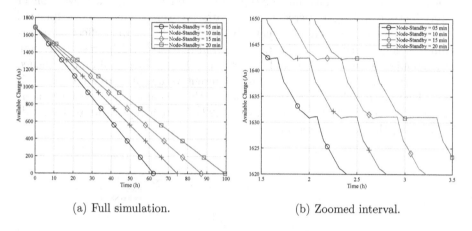

(a) Full simulation.   (b) Zoomed interval.

Fig. 5. Comparison between simulations using different sleep periods.

The battery lifetimes in each situation are: 62.2375 h (NS = 5 min), 74.6383 h (NS = 10 min), 87.0389 h (NS = 15 min), and 99.4389 h (NS = 20 min). Figure 5(b) depicts the behaviour of the simulations with zoom. Note the behaviour of the recovery effect in each situation. In this case, it is possible to note that a sleep period equal to 5 min is not enough since the threshold is not reached. The situations with greater sleep times (15 and 20 min) offer a longer battery lifetime, however, the charge recovery is insignificant as from 10 min. Thus, if the interest lies only in the recovery effect without wasting time, the most suitable task combination is the one that provides a sleep time of 10 min.

5.2   Recovery Effect: Changing the Sleep Period Order

This section performs a variation of the previous simulation. In this case, the sleep period is placed at different moments to evaluate the impact on battery lifetime. The tasks are ordered as follows: NS-Tx-Rx-Ac, Tx-NS-Rx-Ac, Tx-Rx-NS-Ac, and Tx-Rx-Ac-NS. The experiments are performed cyclically until the content in the Available Charge tank reaches the minimum level. Table 3 shows the results, including the charge recovered after a sleep period, at t $\approx$ 36 h.

58   L.M. Rodrigues et al.

Table 3. Results when the sleep period is placed at different moments.

Simulation	Order	Battery lifetime (s)	Battery lifetime (h)	Charge recovered (%)
1	NS-Tx-Rx-Ac	269297	74.8047	0.034
2	Tx-NS-Rx-Ac	269304	74.8067	0.102
3	Tx-Rx-NS-Ac	268698	74.6383	0.065
4	Tx-Rx-Ac-NS	268698	74.6383	0.035

Note that there is a little difference between the times obtained in the simulations. Simulation 2, which has a sleep period after a Tx task, achieved longer battery lifetime and higher percentage of charge recovered. This can be explained by the simple fact that there is a greater benefit with the recovery effect after performing a higher consumption task, as depicted in Fig. 6, which presents a zoom of the simulation final period ($74\,\mathrm{h} \leq t \leq 74.9\,\mathrm{h}$). Simulations 3 and 4 reached the same time, although they presented different values of charge recovered. It may indicate a model inconsistency regarding this situation. The relative difference between the Simulations 2 and 3 is 0.22%, which represents 606 seconds (10.1 min) in the battery lifetime.

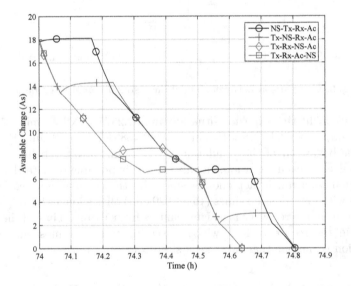

Fig. 6. Simulated experiments with different sleep period order.

5.3 Assessing Changes in Task Execution Order

This section presents a comparison between simulations with different task execution order. The objective is to evaluate the difference in battery lifetime in each situation. In this scenario, the sleep period is not included in the task set. Although there is not a period in sleep mode itself, note that the recovery effect also has its share in this scenario since the tasks present different discharge currents. The tasks are divided as shown in Table 4.

Table 4. Results with different task order.

Simulation	Order	Battery lifetime (s)	Battery lifetime (h)
1	Tx-Rx-Ac	179412	49.8367
2	Tx-Ac-Rx	179586	49.8850
3	Rx-Tx-Ac	179490	49.8583
4	Rx-Ac-Tx	179765	49.9347
5	Ac-Tx-Rx	179576	49.8822
6	Ac-Rx-Tx	179746	49.9294

Note that all simulations have different battery lifetimes, even if the tasks are the same, but in a different execution order. In this case, Simulation 4 showed longer battery lifetime, 179765 s (49.9347 h). The task with the highest discharge current (Tx) is performed lastly in this simulation. On the other hand, Simulation 1 had the shortest battery lifetime, 179412 s (49.8367 h). In this case, the task with the highest discharge current (Tx) is performed first. The relative difference in these two cases (Simulations 1 and 4) is 0.19%, which represents 353 s (5.88 min) in the battery lifetime. Figure 7 depicts a zoom with the last moments of the performed simulations.

5.4 Evaluating Task Switching Frequency

This section evaluates the KiBaM behaviour with regard to the influence of the task switching frequency in battery lifetime. The goal is to establish a frequency range in which the simulation execution time is feasible.

In this scenario, only two tasks are used: Tx and NS. The execution times are defined according to the duty cycle, which in this case is 50%. For example, if the duty cycle period is 16 s, each task runs for 8 s. The simulated frequencies are as follows: 0.015625, 0.03125, 0.0625, 0.125, 0.25, 0.5, 1, 2, 4, 8, 16, 32, and 64 Hz. Table 5 shows the results in each situation.

Note that the battery lifetime is virtually the same within the simulated frequencies range. The differences in battery lifetimes arise due to the simulation step, which is different in each simulated frequency. However, the simulation execution time increases considerably as increases the rate of task switching. We found a linear growth in our simulations. This is due to the increase in the number of iterations required to run the model. That is, the higher the frequency, the lower the amount of charge drained from the battery at each iteration of the

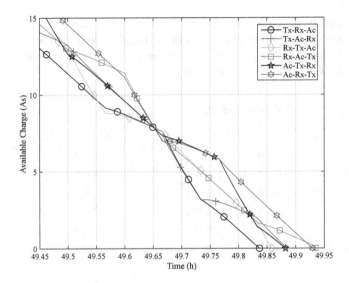

Fig. 7. Simulations with different task order.

Table 5. Results with different frequencies.

Frequency (Hz)	Period (s)	Tasks	Battery lifetime (s)	Battery lifetime (h)	Execution time (s)
0.015625	64.0	Tx-NS	212352.00	58.9867	0.004814
0.03125	32.0	Tx-NS	212352.00	58.9867	0.008408
0.0625	16.0	Tx-NS	212368.00	58.9911	0.016665
0.125	8.0	Tx-NS	212376.00	58.9933	0.029949
0.25	4.0	Tx-NS	212376.00	58.9933	0.054279
0.5	2.0	Tx-NS	212378.00	58.9939	0.108964
1	1.0	Tx-NS	212379.00	58.9942	0.223868
2	0.5	Tx-NS	212379.00	58.9942	0.406734
4	0.25	Tx-NS	212379.25	58.9942	0.812888
8	0.125	Tx-NS	212379.38	58.9943	1.657588
16	0.0625	Tx-NS	212379.50	58.9943	3.262296
32	0.03125	Tx-NS	212379.50	58.9943	6.655759
64	0.015625	Tx-NS	212379.50	58.9943	12.757468

algorithm, and therefore the greater the number of iterations required. This makes the simulation execution time impractical from a certain frequency value since the period of the tasks is too small.

6   Conclusions

The energy constraint is a major challenge within WSN context since it forces network designers to use energy-aware algorithms/protocols to avoid extra costs by replacing batteries. In addition, batteries have intrinsic effects due to electrochemical reactions, which provide energy to the connected device. Two widely studied effects are the rate capacity and charge recovery.

Since batteries are complex devices, the use of battery models assists WSN designers to predict the network behaviour since such models are capable of providing an estimate of the battery lifetime according to the used load profile.

In this paper, we evaluated an analytical battery model, known as KiBaM, to assess the impact of the recovery effect on the battery of low-power WSN nodes. It was possible to verify that the way the recovery effect is used can influence the battery lifetime. Our results presented a difference up to 10.1 min in battery lifetime just by changing the sleep period order. In addition, a minimum standby time (sleep period) is required to achieve a satisfactory charge recovery, i.e., a threshold. For the parameters used in this simulation (discharge currents, execution times, KiBaM constants), a time between 5 and 10 min is enough to recover the battery charge. Finally, we evaluated the frequency of task switching and its impact on the KiBaM execution time. The results showed that higher switching frequencies increase the simulation execution time.

As future work, it is interesting to evaluate the KiBaM through experiments with low-power WSN nodes. In this sense, it is important to consider the battery technology used to adjust the model parameters properly.

Acknowledgement. Authors would like to thank the financial support from CAPES/Brazil, CNPq/Brazil (400508/2014-1, 445700/2014-9), CAPES-FCT (353-13/2012) and FCT/Portugal (Project UID/EMS/50022/2013).

References

1. Akyildiz, I.F., Su, W., Sankarasubramaniam, Y., Cayirci, E.: Wireless sensor networks: a survey. Comput. Netw. **38**, 393–422 (2002)
2. Semprebom, T., Montez, C., Araújo, G., Portugal, P.: A sleep-scheduling scheme for enhancing QoS and network coverage in IEEE 802.15.4 WSN. In: 11th IEEE World Conference on Factory Communication Systems (WFCS), 27–29 May 2015
3. Pinto, A., Camada, M., Dantas, M., Montez, C., Portugal, P., Vasques, F.: Genetic machine learning algorithms in the optimization of communication efficiency in wireless sensor networks. pp. 2448–2453 (2009)
4. Manwell, J.F., McGowan, J.G.: Lead acid battery storage model for hybrid energy systems. Sol. Energy **50**(5), 399–405 (1993)
5. Manwell, J.F., McGowan, J.G.: Extension of the Kinect battery model for wind/hybrid power systems. In: 5th European Wind Energy Association Conference (1994)
6. Rakhmatov, D., Vrudhula, S., Chakrabarti, C.: Battery-conscious task sequencing for portable devices including voltage/clock scaling. In: Proceedings of 2002 Design Automation Conference (IEEE Cat. No. 02CH37324), pp. 189–194 (2002)

7. Rakhmatov, D., Vrudhula, S.: An analytical high-level battery model for use in energy management of portable electronic systems. In: IEEE-ACM International Conference on Computer Aided Design (ICCAD), pp. 488–493 (2002)
8. Rong, P., Pedram, M.: An analytical model for predicting the remaining battery capacity of lithium-ion batteries. IEEE Trans. Very Large Scale Integration (VLSI) Syst. 14(5), 441–451 (2006)
9. Jongerden, M.R., Haverkort, B.R.: Maximizing system lifetime by battery scheduling. In: IEEE/IFIP International Conference on Dependable Systems and Networks (DSN 2009), pp. 63–72 (2009)
10. Chau, C., Wahab, M.H., Qin, F., Wang, Y., Yang, Y.: Battery recovery aware sensor networks. In: Proceedings of 7th International Symposium on Modeling and Optimization in Mobile (WiOPT 2009), Seoul, Korea, pp. 1–9, 23–27 June 2009
11. Rohner, C., Feeney, L.M., Gunningberg, P.: Evaluating battery models in wireless sensor networks. In: 11th International Conference on Wired/Wireless Internet Communication (WWIC 2013), Petersburg, Russia, pp. 29–42, 5–7 June 2013
12. Daniil, N., Drury, D., Mellor, P.H.: Performance comparison of diffusion, circuit-based and kinetic battery models. In: IEEE Energy Conversion Congress and Exposition (ECCE 2015), pp. 1382–1389, 20–24 September 2015
13. Rodrigues, L.M., Montez, C., Moraes, R., Vasques, F., Portugal, P.: A temperature dependent battery model for wireless sensor networks. Sensors 17, 422 (2017)
14. Dusza, B., Marwedel, P., Spinczyk, O., Wietfeld, C.: A context-aware battery lifetime model for carrier aggregation enabled LTE-A systems. In: IEEE 11th Consumer Communications and Networking Conference (CCNC 2014), pp. 13–19 (2014)
15. Yurur, O., Liu, C., Moreno, W.: Modeling battery behavior on sensory operations for context-aware smartphone sensing. Sensors 15(6), 12:323–12:341 (2015)
16. Kaj, I., Konané, V.: Modeling battery cells under discharge using kinetic and stochastic battery models. Appl. Math. Model. 40(17–18), 7901–7915 (2016)
17. Jongerden, M.R.: Model-based energy analysis of battery powered systems. Ph.D. dissertation, University of Twente, Enschede, December 2010. http://doc.utwente.nl/75079/
18. Jongerden, M.R., Haverkort, B.R.: Battery modeling. Technical report, University of Twente (2008)
19. Schneider, K.K., Sausen, P.S., Sausen, A.: Análise Comparativa do Tempo de Vida de Baterias em Dispositivos Móveis a Partir da Utilização de Modelos Analíticos. Tendências em Matemática Aplicada e Computacional 12(1), 43–54 (2011)
20. Manwell, J.F., McGowan, J.G., Baring-Gould, E., Stein, W., Leotta, A.: Evaluation of battery models for wind/hybrid power systems simulation. In: 5th European Wind Energy Association Conference, pp. 1182–1187 (1994)
21. Jongerden, M.R., Haverkort, B.R.: Which battery to use? In: 24th UK Performance Engineering Workshop, pp. 76–88 (2008)
22. Gandolfo, D., Brandão, A., Patiño, D., Molina, M.: Dynamic model of lithium polymer battery - load resistor method for electric parameters identification. J. Energy Inst. 88(4), 470–479 (2015)
23. Mikhaylov, K., Tervonen, J.: Experimental evaluation of alkaline batteries's capacity for low power consuming applications. In: Proceedings of 7th IEEE International Conference on Advanced Information Networking and Applications (AINA 2012), Fukuoka, Japan, pp. 331–337, 26–29 March 2012

3D Path-Following Algorithms for Unmanned Aerial Vehicles Adjusted with Genetic Algorithm

Guilherme V. Pelizer, Natassya B.F. Silva$^{(\boxtimes)}$, and Kalinka R.L.J.C. Branco

Universidade de São Paulo (USP), Avenida Trabalhador São-carlense, 400, São Carlos, SP 13566-590, Brazil
guilherme.pelizer@usp.br, naty.ays@gmail.com

Abstract. Unmanned Aerial Vehicle (UAV) is a growing research topic due to its wide range of applications. One of its major challenges is the development of the autopilot, responsible for keeping the aircraft in desired flight conditions and for executing navigation tasks. A navigation task that is usually necessary is the path-following, which guarantees that the aircraft follows a predefined trajectory. It is possible to find several approaches for this function, based in geometric and control techniques; however, compared only for the 2D scenario. Therefore, this paper objective is to present new extended path-following algorithms for the 3D scenario, based in the well-known path-following algorithms Lookahead, Non-Linear Guidance Law (NLGL), Pure Pursuit and Line-of-Sight (PLOS) and Vector Field. The algorithms parameters are obtained with Genetic Algorithm optimisation and a comparison between all of them is performed in an environment with and without wind. The results from the simulations show that Vector Field has the best performance and PLOS has the worse one due to a high effort demanded.

Keywords: Path-following algorithms · Genetic Algorithm · Unmanned Aerial Vehicles

1 Introduction

Unmanned Aerial Vehicles (UAVs) are machines that can fly without a human aboard and can operate autonomously or can be remotely piloted. One important element of an autonomous UAV is the autopilot, which is responsible for keeping the aircraft in desired flight conditions and for executing navigation tasks, like following a trajectory [4]. The path-following functionality is essential most applications, such as environmental monitoring, roads and railways mapping, fire detection and prevention, and search and rescue in disasters [1,18].

The literature on path-following algorithms for UAVs shows a variety of approaches that combine geometric and control techniques, like pure pursuit [17], Line-of-Sight (LOS) [5], non-linear control [8] and vector fields [7]. Given the diversity of choices, it is a hard decision to choose between them. As a

© Springer International Publishing AG 2017
K. Branco et al. (Eds.): WoCCES 2013-2016, CCIS 702, pp. 63–80, 2017.
DOI: 10.1007/978-3-319-61403-8_4

possible solution, Sujit et al. [13,14] presented a comparison between a subset of path-following algorithms. However, a major drawback from their study is to consider only a two dimensional (2D) scenario.

The path-following problem in a 3D scenario is to find the commanded yaw and pitch angles, ψ_d and θ_d, and consequently their rates, q_d and r_d, to guarantee that the aircraft follows a predefined trajectory. The information that is available for the autopilot to fulfil this task is the aircraft current position, $\boldsymbol{p} = [x, y, z]^T$ in an inertial frame, its current yaw and pitch angles, ψ and θ and the desired trajectory. The trajectory analysed in this paper is represented by a list of way-points, $\boldsymbol{W_i}$ and $\boldsymbol{W_{i+1}}$ that define straight lines. Therefore, the problem results in minimising the distance between the position and the trajectory line. Moreover, a good solution must be accurate and provide feasible efforts for an UAV with physical constraints.

In this context, since UAVs applications usually benefit from its natural three dimensional (3D) movement, it is important to analyse path-following algorithms in this scenario rather than 2D scenario. Thus, this paper objective is to present new 3D extended path-following algorithms, based in the algorithms Lookahead [2], Non-Linear Guidance Law (NLGL) [11], Pure Pursuit and Line-of-Sight (PLOS) [16] and Vector Field [10]. Moreover, comparisons of these new algorithms with their best configuration parameters obtained with GA are performed in a simulation environment with and without wind disturbances.

2 Kinematic Modelling

In normal conditions during a stabilised flight with a constant velocity intensity, v, the aircraft movement can be described by its kinematic modelling [15].

$$\dot{x} = v \cos (\psi) \cos (\theta) \tag{1}$$
$$\dot{y} = v \sin (\psi) \cos (\theta) \tag{2}$$
$$\dot{z} = -v \sin (\theta) \tag{3}$$
$$q = \dot{\theta} \tag{4}$$
$$r = \dot{\psi} \tag{5}$$

However, when we consider a flight that is affected by a wind with intensity v_w and direction ψ_w, the aircraft velocity is directly disturbed, resulting in a kinematic modelling represented by (6)–(10) [13].

$$\dot{x} = v \cos (\psi) \cos (\theta) + v_w \cos (\psi_w) \tag{6}$$
$$\dot{y} = v \sin (\psi) \cos (\theta) + v_w \sin (\psi_w) \tag{7}$$
$$\dot{z} = -v \sin (\theta) \tag{8}$$
$$q = \dot{\theta} \tag{9}$$
$$r = \dot{\psi} \tag{10}$$

3   3D Path-Following Algorithms

New 3D path-following algorithms were designed with an extension of well-known 2D algorithms, Lookahead [2], Non-Linear Guidance Law (NLGL) [11], Pure Pursuit and Line-of-Sight (PLOS) [16] and Vector Field [10]. The extension process involves the definition of two frames in addition to the inertial frame, a path frame and an intermediate frame. The path frame represents the frame whose X_p axis has the desired velocity direction that would keep the aircraft in the desired trajectory.

The inertial frame, represented by axis X_i, Y_i and Z_i, is an Earth-fixed tangential frame in local-level and tangent to the gravity. The intermediate frame, represented by axis X', Y' and Z', is the frame resulted from an α rotation in the Z_i axis of the inertial frame and the path frame, represented by axis X_p, Y_p and Z_p, is the result of a β rotation in the Y' axis of the intermediate frame, as illustrated in Fig. 1.

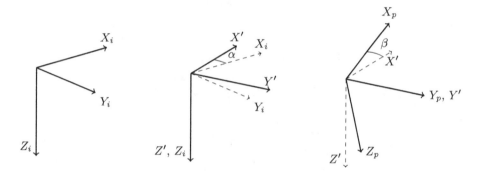

Fig. 1. Inertial, intermediate and path frames and the rotations to derive them.

With the path frame specification well established, it is useful to define the error vector as (11), where $R_Z(\alpha)$ is the rotation matrix from the inertial frame to the intermediate frame defined by (12) and $R_{Y'}(\beta)$ is the rotation matrix from the intermediate frame to the path frame defined by (13). The angles α and β are calculated as (14) and (15) respectively, using the waypoints $W_i = [x_i, y_i, z_i]^T$ and $W_{i+1} = [x_{i+1}, y_{i+1}, z_{i+1}]^T$ that specify a straight line trajectory and their rotated equivalents $W_i^R = R_Z(\alpha) W_i = [x_i^R, y_i^R, z_i^R]^T$ and $W_{i+1}^R = R_Z(\alpha) W_{i+1} = [x_{i+1}^R, y_{i+1}^R, z_{i+1}^R]^T$.

$$e = R_{Y'}(\beta) R_Z(\alpha)(p - W_i) \tag{11}$$

$$R_Z(\alpha) = \begin{pmatrix} \cos(\alpha) & -\sin(\alpha) & 0 \\ \sin(\alpha) & \cos(\alpha) & 0 \\ 0 & 0 & 1 \end{pmatrix} \tag{12}$$

$$\boldsymbol{R_{Y'}}(\beta) = \begin{pmatrix} \cos(\beta) & 0 & \sin(\beta) \\ 0 & 1 & 0 \\ -\sin(\beta) & 1 & \cos(\beta) \end{pmatrix} \tag{13}$$

$$\alpha = arctan\left(\frac{y_{i+1} - y_i}{x_{i+1} - x_i}\right) \tag{14}$$

$$\beta = arctan\left(\frac{z_i^R - z_{i+1}^R}{\sqrt{\left(x_{i+1}^R - x_i^R\right)^2 + \left(y_{i+1}^R - y_i^R\right)^2}}\right) \tag{15}$$

The error vector components in the path frame, $\boldsymbol{e} = [e_x, e_y, e_z]^T$, defines the along-track error e_x, the cross-track error e_y and the vertical-track error e_z, as can be seen in Fig. 2 [2].

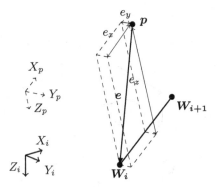

Fig. 2. The error vector $\boldsymbol{e}$ and its respective components e_x, e_y and e_z represented in the path frame.

Therefore, the objectives of the new 3D path-following algorithms are to reduce the components cross-track error e_y and vertical-track error e_z by commanding the yaw rate r and pitch rate q of the aircraft. The reduction of these errors implies an approximation to the desired trajectory defined by a straight line. It is also important that the aircraft arrives at the desired trajectory before it reaches the next waypoint, otherwise the convergence of the path-following algorithms can not be guaranteed.

Since the error vector is defined from the waypoint $\boldsymbol{W_i}$, it is natural that the along-track error e_x increases as the aircraft gets close to the next waypoint $\boldsymbol{W_{i+1}}$ and that is why it is not considered in the algorithms. This strategy was chosen to improve the fairness when comparing all algorithms methods with a fixed desired point to represent the line.

Each algorithm, which are the result of the extension process, uses its own control laws and has specific parameters, as presented in the following subsections.

3.1 Lookahead

The Lookahead path-following algorithm uses the concept of virtual target to guarantee that the aircraft follows a desired trajectory [2]. The virtual target is set as a goal point to where the aircraft should be directed to. On the Lookahead approach, the point location is at a fixed distance, called lookahead distance. With the extension process, we can define two lookahead distances, one represented by δ_y in the X_P axis and another one represented by δ_z in the X' axis.

The extended Lookahead algorithms starts with the control laws (16)–(17), which guarantee the convergence of the algorithm, where δ_y and δ_z respectively drive the position to the $X_P Y_P$ and $X_P Z_P$ planes. Then, the angular velocities are obtained with proportional gains k_ψ and k_θ. Algorithm 1 summarises all the steps of the Looakhead algorithm for the 3D path following.

$$\psi_d = \alpha + arctan\left(\frac{-e_y}{\delta_y}\right) \tag{16}$$

$$\theta_d = \beta + arctan\left(\frac{e_z}{\delta_z}\right) \tag{17}$$

Algorithm 1. Lookahead algorithm.

1: **function** LOOKAHEAD($\boldsymbol{W_i} = [x_i, y_i, z_i]^T$, $\boldsymbol{W_{i+1}} = [x_{i+1}, y_{i+1}, z_{i+1}]^T$, $\boldsymbol{p} = [x, y, z]^T$, ψ, θ, δ_y, δ_z, k_ψ, k_θ)

2: $\quad \alpha \leftarrow arctan\left(\frac{y_{i+1}-y_i}{x_{i+1}-x_i}\right)$

3: $\quad \triangleright \boldsymbol{W_i^R} = \left[x_i^R, y_i^R, z_i^R\right]^T$

4: $\quad \boldsymbol{W_i^R} \leftarrow \boldsymbol{R_z}(\alpha) \boldsymbol{W_i}$

5: $\quad \triangleright \boldsymbol{W_{i+1}^R} = \left[x_{i+1}^R, y_{i+1}^R, z_{i+1}^R\right]^T$

6: $\quad \boldsymbol{W_{i+1}^R} \leftarrow \boldsymbol{R_z}(\alpha) \boldsymbol{W_{i+1}}$

7: $\quad \beta \leftarrow arctan\left(\frac{z_i^R - z_{i+1}^R}{x_{i+1}^R - x_i^R}\right)$

8: $\quad \triangleright \boldsymbol{e} = [e_x, e_y, e_z]^T$

9: $\quad \boldsymbol{e} = \boldsymbol{R_y}(\beta) \boldsymbol{R_z}(\alpha)(\boldsymbol{p} - \boldsymbol{W_i})$

10: $\quad \psi_d \leftarrow \alpha + arctan\left(\frac{-e_y}{\delta_y}\right)$

11: $\quad \theta_d \leftarrow \beta + arctan\left(\frac{e_z}{\delta_z}\right)$

12: $\quad r_d \leftarrow k_\psi(\psi_d - \psi)$

13: $\quad q_d \leftarrow k_\theta(\theta_d - \theta)$

14: $\quad$ **return** (r_d, q_d)

15: **end function**

A preliminary analysis of the gain parameters shows that low values of δ_y, δ_z, k_ψ and k_θ result in trajectories with high overshoot oscillations and high values produce responses without overshoot but with high settling time.

3.2   Non-Linear Guidance Law

The Non-Linear Guidance Law (NLGL) also uses the concept of virtual target by calculating the interception between the trajectory and a circle with a fixed radius from the aircraft position. The extension process was already applied to the NLGL algorithm, with the yaw rate and pitch rate obtained from the control laws (18)–(19), where L_ψ is the radius for the circle in the XY plane, L_θ is the radius for the circle in the $X'Z'$ plane, η_ψ is the angle that directs the aircraft to the trajectory in the $X_P Y_P$ plane and η_θ is the angle that directs the aircraft to the trajectory in the $X_P Z_P$ plane [12].

$$r_d = 2\frac{v^2}{L_\psi}\sin\left(\eta_\psi\right) \tag{18}$$

$$q_d = 2\frac{v^2}{L_\theta}\sin\left(\eta_\theta\right) \tag{19}$$

The results of the extended algorithm NLGL for the 3D scenario show an effective response to a straight line trajectory for $L_\psi = 20$ m and $L_\theta = 20$ m [12]. However, this algorithm version still have implementation issues, such as failing to find the interception between the trajectory line and the circle for some cases and having oscillatory responses due to too large angles of η_ψ and η_θ. To overcome these limitations, an improved new algorithm can be implemented, called NLGL$_+$.

In the NLGL$_+$, if the algorithm does not find an interception between the line and the circle, the radius used in that iteration specifically is the smallest distance between the aircraft and the trajectory. Another improvement is to establish a maximum interception angle of $\pi/4$ [3]. The complete algorithm can be seen in Algorithm 2.

A simple experiment was performed to compare the previous extended version of NLGL and its improved version, NLGL$_+$. By using the same trajectory reported in [12], with waypoints $\boldsymbol{W_0} = [0,0,0]^T$ and $\boldsymbol{W_1} = [150, 150, 150]^T$, same kinematic model and aircraft conditions, we executed the NLGL$_+$ for different values of L_ψ and L_θ and calculated the RMS of the module of the error considering only the cross-track error and vertical-track error. First, L_θ was fixed in 13 m and L_ψ assumed different values, as can be seen in Table 1. Then, L_ψ was fixed in 13 m and L_θ assumed different values, as can be seen in Table 2.

Table 1. RMS of the error for algorithm NLGL$_+$ with $L_\theta = 13$ m and different values of L_ψ.

L_ψ (m)	10	11	12	13	14	15	20	25	30
Error RMS (m)	5.6487	5.2739	5.0448	4.9780	5.0491	5.1296	5.5686	6.1305	6.2215

Algorithm 2. Improved Non-Linear Guidance Law Algorithm.

1: **function** $\mathrm{NLGL}(W_i = [x_i, y_i, z_i]^T,\ W_{i+1} = [x_{i+1}, y_{i+1}, z_{i+1}]^T,\ p = [x, y, z]^T,\ \psi,$
   $\theta,\ v,\ L_\psi,\ L_\theta)$

2:      $\alpha \leftarrow \arctan\left(\frac{y_{i+1}-y_i}{x_{i+1}-x_i}\right)$

3:      ▷ Calculates intersection between circle of radius L_ψ and line with points W_i
        and W_{i+1} in xy plane.

4:      ▷ $p_{vt,\psi} = [x_{vt,\psi}, y_{vt,\psi}, z_{vt,\psi}]^T$

5:      $p_{vt,\psi} \leftarrow Intersection\_xy\,(L_\psi, W_i, W_{i+1})$

6:      ▷ $W_i^R = [x_i^R, y_i^R, z_i^R]^T$

7:      $W_i^R \leftarrow R_z\,(\alpha)\,W_i$

8:      ▷ $W_{i+1}^R = [x_{i+1}^R, y_{i+1}^R, z_{i+1}^R]^T$

9:      $W_{i+1}^R \leftarrow R_z\,(\alpha)\,W_{i+1}$

10:     ▷ Calculates intersection between circle of radius L_θ and line with points W_i^R
        and W_{i+1}^R in xz plane.

11:     ▷ $p_{vt,\theta} = [x_{vt,\theta}, y_{vt,\theta}, z_{vt,\theta}]^T$

12:     $p_{vt,\theta} \leftarrow Intersection\_xz\,(L_\theta, W_i^R, W_{i+1}^R)$

13:     $\sigma_\psi \leftarrow \arctan\left(\frac{y_{vt,\psi}-y}{x_{vt,\psi}-x}\right)$

14:     $\sigma_\theta \leftarrow \arctan\left(\frac{z-z_{vt,\theta}}{x_{vt,\theta}-x}\right)$

15:     $\eta_\psi \leftarrow \psi - \sigma_\psi$

16:     **if** $\eta_\psi > \pi/4$ **then**

17:         $\eta_\psi \leftarrow \pi/4$

18:     **end if**

19:     $\eta_\theta \leftarrow \theta - \sigma_\theta$

20:     **if** $\eta_\theta > \pi/4$ **then**

21:         $\eta_\theta \leftarrow \pi/4$

22:     **end if**

23:     $r_d \leftarrow 2\frac{v^2}{L_\psi}\sin(\eta_\psi)$

24:     $q_d \leftarrow 2\frac{v^2}{L_\theta}\sin(\eta_\theta)$

25:     **return** (r_d, q_d)

26: **end function**

Table 2. RMS of the error for algorithm $\mathrm{NLGL_+}$ with $L_\psi = 13$ m and different values of L_θ.

L_θ (m)	10	11	12	13	14	15	20	25	30
Error RMS (m)	4.9821	4.9750	4.9747	4.9780	4.9820	4.9874	5.0183	5.0507	5.0874

The error RMS of the previous version of extended NLGL for its best parameter configuration ($L_\psi = 20$ and $L_\theta = 20$) is 5.3734 m, while the error RMS of the best parameter configuration ($L_\psi = 13$ and $L_\theta = 12$) of $\mathrm{NLGL_+}$ is 4.9747 m. We were able to use smaller values for L_θ and L_ψ in $\mathrm{NLGL_+}$ due to absence of the geometric limitation, which, together with limited η_ψ and η_θ, resulted in a faster convergence to the straight line trajectory and smaller errors. Therefore, since $\mathrm{NLGL_+}$ shows better results than its previous version, it is chosen to be used as representative for comparison with the other methods.

3.3   Pure Pursuit and Line-of-Sight

The Pure Pursuit and Line-of-Sight (PLOS) algorithm is composed of two strategies. The first, Line-of-Sight (LOS) guidance, is responsible for decreasing the position error with respect to the desired trajectory, while the second one, pure pursuit, drives the aircraft to the next waypoint by adjusting the angle direction [16].

In the extension process, both strategies are adapted, considering the cross-track error and vertical-track error for the LOS part and the desired angles as α and β for the pure pursuit part. The resulting control laws are defined as (20) for the convergence in the $X_P Y_P$ plane and as (21) for the convergence in the $X_P Z_P$ plane, where $k_{PP,\psi}$ and $k_{PP,\theta}$ are the proportional gains of the pure pursuit strategy and $k_{LOS,\psi}$ and $k_{LOS,\theta}$ are the proportional gains of the LOS strategy. Algorithm 3 describes all calculations of the extended PLOS algorithm.

$$r_d = k_{PP,\psi} \left(\psi_d - \psi \right) + k_{LOS,\psi} \left(-e_y \right) \tag{20}$$

$$q_d = k_{PP,\theta} \left(\theta_d - \theta \right) + k_{LOS,\theta} \left(e_z \right) \tag{21}$$

Algorithm 3. Pure Pursuit and Line-of-Sight algorithm.

1: **function** PLOS($W_i = [x_i, y_i, z_i]^T$, $W_{i+1} = [x_{i+1}, y_{i+1}, z_{i+1}]^T$, $p = [x, y, z]^T$, ψ, θ, $k_{PP,\psi}$, $k_{LOS,\psi}$, $k_{PP,\theta}$, $k_{LOS,\theta}$)

2:      $\alpha \leftarrow arctan\left(\frac{y_{i+1} - y_i}{x_{i+1} - x_i} \right)$

3:      $\psi_d \leftarrow \alpha$

4:      $\triangleright$ $W_i^R = \left[x_i^R, y_i^R, z_i^R \right]^T$

5:      $W_i^R \leftarrow R_z \left(\alpha \right) W_i$

6:      $\triangleright$ $W_{i+1}^R = \left[x_{i+1}^R, y_{i+1}^R, z_{i+1}^R \right]^T$

7:      $W_{i+1}^R \leftarrow R_z \left(\alpha \right) W_{i+1}$

8:      $\triangleright$ $p^R = \left[x^R, y^R, z^R \right]^T$

9:      $p^R \leftarrow R_z \left(\alpha \right) p$

10:     $\beta \leftarrow arctan\left(\frac{z_i^R - z_{i+1}^R}{x_{i+1}^R - x_i^R} \right)$

11:     $\theta_d \leftarrow \beta$

12:     $\triangleright$ $e = [e_x, e_y, e_z]^T$

13:     $e = R_y \left(\beta \right) R_z \left(\alpha \right) \left(p - W_i \right)$

14:     $r_d \leftarrow k_{PP,\psi} \left(\psi_d - \psi \right) + k_{LOS,\psi} \left(-e_y \right)$

15:     $q_d \leftarrow k_{PP,\theta} \left(\theta_d - \theta \right) + k_{LOS,\theta} \left(e_z \right)$

16:     **return** (r_d, q_d)

17: **end function**

In the extended PLOS algorithm, one strategy can predominate over the other, according to the relation between the pure pursuit gain and the LOS gain. For this reason, besides finding values that give satisfactory responses, it is also important to find a balance between the gains.

An initial analysis of the parameters show that low values of $k_{PP,\psi}$ and $k_{PP,\theta}$ leads to oscillatory trajectories that may not converge, while high values lead to high settling time. In the case of high values of $k_{LOS,\psi}$ and $k_{LOS,\theta}$ the trajectory has overshoot, while for low values it converges too slowly.

3.4   Vector Field

The Vector Field path-following algorithm uses the notion of vector fields that are directed toward the desired trajectory and indicates the desired direction of flight. The original Vector Field algorithm uses sliding mode approach to define the trajectory desired course and demonstrate the convergence of the control law in the presence of wind disturbances with Lyapunov stability arguments [10].

The resulting control laws from the extension process for the Vector Field algorithm are (22) and (23), where χ_ψ^∞ and χ_θ^∞ are the maximum angles of approach to the trajectory; ϵ_ψ and ϵ_θ are the width of the transition region around the sliding surface that reduces the chatter in the control; s_ψ and s_θ are positive constants that influence the rate of transition of the desired angle from $\chi_{\psi,\theta}^\infty$ to 0; $\tilde{\chi}_\psi$ and $\tilde{\chi}_\theta$ are the desired course of the vector field defined, respectively, by (24) for the $X_P Y_P$ plane and by (25) for the $X_P Z_P$ plane; and $sat(x)$ is the saturation function defined in (26) and used to avoid adverse affects of chattering. The parameters k_ψ and k_θ are gains of the yaw rate and pitch rate proportional controllers, as can be seen in Algorithm 4.

$$\psi_d = \psi - \frac{\chi_\psi^\infty}{k_\psi} \frac{2}{\pi} \frac{s_\psi v \sin(\psi)}{1 - (s_\psi e_y)^2} - \frac{\kappa_\psi}{k_\psi} sat\left(\frac{\tilde{\chi}_\psi}{\epsilon_\psi}\right) \tag{22}$$

$$\theta_d = \theta - \frac{\chi_\theta^\infty}{k_\theta} \frac{2}{\pi} \frac{s_\theta v \sin(\theta)}{1 - (s_\theta e_z)^2} - \frac{\kappa_\theta}{k_\theta} sat\left(\frac{\tilde{\chi}_\theta}{\epsilon_\theta}\right) \tag{23}$$

$$\tilde{\chi}_\psi = \psi - \left(-\chi_\psi^\infty \frac{2}{\pi} arctan\left(s_\psi e_y\right)\right) \tag{24}$$

$$\tilde{\chi}_\theta = \theta - \left(-\chi_\theta^\infty \frac{2}{\pi} arctan\left(s_\theta e_y\right)\right) \tag{25}$$

$$sat(x) = \begin{cases} x, & \text{if } |x| \leq 1 \\ 1, & \text{if } |x| > 1 \text{ and } x > 0 \\ 0, & \text{if } |x| > 1 \text{ and } x = 0 \\ -1, & \text{if } |x| > 1 \text{ and } x < 0 \end{cases} \tag{26}$$

Algorithm 4. Vector Field algorithm.

1: **function** VECTOR_FIELD($\boldsymbol{W_i} = [x_i, y_i, z_i]^T$, $\boldsymbol{W_{i+1}} = [x_{i+1}, y_{i+1}, z_{i+1}]^T$, $\boldsymbol{p} =$ $[x, y, z]^T$, ψ, θ, v, χ_ψ^∞, k_ψ, s_ψ, κ_ψ, ϵ_ψ, χ_θ^∞, k_θ, s_θ, κ_θ, ϵ_θ)

2:    $\alpha \leftarrow arctan\left(\frac{y_{i+1}-y_i}{x_{i+1}-x_i}\right)$

3:    ▷ $\boldsymbol{W_i^R} = \left[x_i^R, y_i^R, z_i^R\right]^T$

4:    $\boldsymbol{W_i^R} \leftarrow \boldsymbol{R_z}\left(\alpha\right)\boldsymbol{W_i}$

5:    ▷ $\boldsymbol{W_{i+1}^R} = \left[x_{i+1}^R, y_{i+1}^R, z_{i+1}^R\right]^T$

6:    $\boldsymbol{W_{i+1}^R} \leftarrow \boldsymbol{R_z}\left(\alpha\right)\boldsymbol{W_{i+1}}$

7:    $\beta \leftarrow arctan\left(\frac{z_i^R-z_{i+1}^R}{x_{i+1}^R-x_i^R}\right)$

8:    ▷ $\boldsymbol{e} = [e_x, e_y, e_z]^T$

9:    $\boldsymbol{e} = \boldsymbol{R_y}\left(\beta\right)\boldsymbol{R_z}\left(\alpha\right)\left(\boldsymbol{p} - \boldsymbol{W_i}\right)$

10:    $\psi_R \leftarrow \psi - \alpha$

11:    $\theta_R \leftarrow \theta - \beta$

12:    $\tilde{\chi}_\psi \leftarrow \psi_R - \left(-\chi_\psi^\infty \frac{2}{\pi} arctan\left(s_\psi e_y\right)\right)$

13:    $\tilde{\chi}_\theta \leftarrow \theta_R - \left(-\chi_\theta^\infty \frac{2}{\pi} arctan\left(s_\theta e_y\right)\right)$

14:    $\psi_d \leftarrow \psi_R - \frac{\chi_\psi^\infty}{k_\psi} \frac{2}{\pi} \frac{s_\psi v \sin(\psi)}{1-\left(s_\psi e_y\right)^2} - \frac{\kappa_\psi}{k_\psi} sat\left(\frac{\tilde{\chi}_\psi}{\epsilon_\psi}\right)$

15:    $\theta_d \leftarrow \theta_R - \frac{\chi_\theta^\infty}{k_\theta} \frac{2}{\pi} \frac{s_\theta v \sin(\theta)}{1-(s_\theta e_z)^2} - \frac{\kappa_\theta}{k_\theta} sat\left(\frac{\tilde{\chi}_\theta}{\epsilon_\theta}\right)$

16:    $\psi_d \leftarrow \psi_d + \alpha$

17:    $\theta_d \leftarrow \theta_d + \beta$

18:    $r_d \leftarrow k_\psi\left(\psi_d - \psi\right)$

19:    $q_d \leftarrow k_\theta\left(\theta_d - \theta\right)$

20:    **return** (r_d, q_d)

21: **end function**

The stability of the Vector Field algorithm is proved for $\chi_{\psi,\theta}^\infty \leq \pi/2$ and large values of it implies in faster convergence toward the path, so it can be set as $\pi/2$. Another parameter that can be set is $\epsilon_{\psi,\theta}$, which is only responsible for reducing the control chatter, so can be set as 1. However, the other control parameters define the shape of the sliding surface and the resulting trajectory and should be correctly chosen to avoid overshoot with large gains and to avoid slow convergence with small gains.

All path-following algorithms extended for the 3D scenario have parameters that are not straightforward to determine. Therefore, it must be found values that could result in responses without overshoot and that converges rapidly to the desired straight line trajectory.

4   Parameters Adjustment

In order to adjust the parameters of each 3D path-following algorithm, it is employed an optimisation procedure based on Genetic Algorithm (GA). The GA method is chosen due to its ability to avoid multiple local optimum solutions by searching through a wide domain and the modularity of its implementation [9].

The GA is an iterative process that uses the concepts of mutations, crossover and selection to find solutions for an optimisation problem. It evolves populations, which are possible solutions, by considering how fit they are in each iteration. The fitness is predetermined by an objective function that defines the problem itself.

In the path-following problem, we can evaluate a solution according to the cross-track error e_y and vertical-track error e_z of a given trajectory, which must be collectively minimised. It is also important to consider the effort for performing the manoeuvres for an aircraft, which in the kinematic modelling are proportional to the commanded yaw and pitch rate. Therefore, the objective function must associate the trajectory error and the aircraft effort.

The error in each iteration of a path-following simulation can be expressed by the norm of an vector composed by the cross-track error and vertical-track error, as in (27). Thus, the error for a complete trajectory can be represented by its RMS, calculated with (28).

$$path\_error_i = \sqrt{e_{y,i}{}^2 + e_{z,i}{}^2} \tag{27}$$

$$e_{RMS} = \sqrt{\frac{1}{N} \sum_{i=1}^{i=N} path\_error_i{}^2} \tag{28}$$

Since the efforts are proportional to the pitch and yaw rates, the efforts for a complete trajectory can be calculated as the mean of their values from each iteration, resulting in (29) and (30).

$$\omega_q = \frac{1}{N} \sum_{i=1}^{i=N} q_i \tag{29}$$

$$\omega_r = \frac{1}{N} \sum_{i=1}^{i=N} r_i \tag{30}$$

The objective function can be specified as (31), where M defines a metric that must be minimised, W_e is a weight for the error part, W_ω is a weight for the effort part, $e_{RMS,max}$ is the maximum value of e_{RMS}, $\omega_{q,max}$ is the maximum value of ω_q and $\omega_{r,max}$ is the maximum value of ω_r. The maximum values are used for normalisation of each metric component to guarantee a fair balance between different physical measurements. It was also considered to use different weights for the error part and the effort part to add flexibility to the metric and to reflect design requirements.

$$M = W_e \left(\frac{e_{RMS}}{e_{RMS,max}} \right) + W_\omega 0.5 \left(\frac{\omega_q}{\omega_{q,max}} + \frac{\omega_r}{\omega_{r,max}} \right) \tag{31}$$

Therefore, a set of parameters for each 3D extended path-following algorithm can be obtained with GA by minimising the metric M. In this way, it is possible to determine the best parameters configuration for each path-following algorithm with a same procedure.

5   Comparison Results

This section presents the results of the best parameters configuration obtained with the GA for each 3D extended path-following algorithms. It is also shown a comparison between all algorithms in the presence and absence of wind disturbances. The simulation environment based on the kinematic modelling, the algorithms and the parameters adjustment procedure were implemented in MATLAB®.

5.1   Optimisation Procedure

The parameters of the path-following algorithms were set with the GA, as described in Sect. 4, for the kinematic modelling without wind presented in (1)–(5). To represent a more realistic scenario for an aircraft with physical constraints, the pitch and yaw rates were limited as $\|q\| < 0.19\,\mathrm{rad/s}$ and $\|r\| < 0.33\,\mathrm{rad/s}$ [13]. Moreover, it is assumed that the commanded pitch and yaw rates are immediately performed by the aircraft when smaller than their limited values, which is appropriate because an inner loop with higher frequency in the autopilot could guarantee its execution.

The trajectory used to optimise the parameters was defined by the following list of waypoints: $W_0 = [0, 0, 0]^T$, $W_1 = [0, 500, 0]^T$, $W_2 = [500, 500, 500]^T$, $W_3 = [500, 0, 500]^T$ and $W_4 = [0, 0, 0]^T$. The initial position of the aircraft was $p = [5, 30, 20]^T$ with $\theta = 0$, $\psi = 0$ and a constant velocity during the whole execution of $v = 15\,\mathrm{m/s}$.

The GA was executed with the ga function from the Global Optimization Toolbox to minimise the objective function defined in (31), with $W_e = 0.7$, $W_\omega = 0.3$ and $e_{RMS,max} = 20\,\mathrm{m}$, $\omega_{q,max} = 0.2\,\mathrm{rad/s}$ and $\omega_{r,max} = 0.2\,\mathrm{rad/s}$. The GA was configured with a population size of 50 individuals and a tolerance function of 10^{-4}. The resulting parameters for each 3D extended path-following algorithm can be seen in Table 3.

Table 3. Best parameter configuration obtained with GA for the objective function (31) for all 3D extended path-following algorithms.

Algorithm	Parameters
Lookahead	$\delta_y = 21.81$ m, $k_\psi = 33.19$ $\delta_z = 66.87$ m, $k_\theta = 105.71$
PLOS	$k_{PP,\psi} = 125.39$, $k_{LOS,\psi} = 5.49$ $k_{PP,\theta} = 447.43$, $k_{LOS,\theta} = 67.19$
NLGL+	$L_\psi = 22.50$ m, $L_\theta = 83.60$ m
Vector Field	$\chi_\psi^\infty = \pi/2$, $\epsilon_\psi = 1$, $k_\psi = 2.22$, $s_\psi = 0.11$, $\kappa_\psi = 0.67$ $\chi_\theta^\infty = \pi/2$, $\epsilon_\theta = 1$, $k_\theta = 3.10$, $s_\theta = 0.04$, $\kappa_\theta = 7.06$

Figure 3 presents the trajectories produced for each algorithm, with their best parameters from Table 3, for the same conditions without wind used for the parameters adjustment. The overall results show that the algorithms are effective and behave similarly in the steady response. Moreover, it can be inferred that PLOS directs the aircraft more quickly to the desired trajectory but its response has oscillations that undermines its correctness.

The errors and efforts normalised and the corresponding metric for each algorithm executing the trajectories represented in Fig. 3 can be seen in Table 4. The best performance, according to the metric, is achieved by Vector Field, followed by Lookahead and NLGL$_+$. PLOS has the higher metric due to an increased effort from the yaw and pitch rates.

The algorithms error RMS are very close to each other, which also happens to the q effort and r effort for Lookahead, NLGL$_+$ and Vector Field. Only PLOS

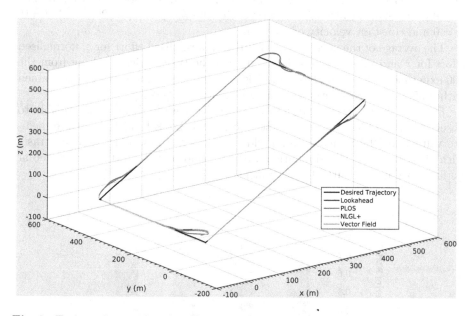

Fig. 3. Trajectories produced without wind for each 3D extended path-following algorithm with their best parameters from Table 3.

Table 4. Error, effort and metric for each algorithm executing the trajectories represented in Fig. 3 without wind.

Algorithm	Normalised error RMS	Normalised effort for q	Normalised effort for r	Metric M
Lookahead	0.66	0.11	0.39	0.54
PLOS	0.65	0.93	0.42	0.66
NLGL$_+$	0.66	0.11	0.38	0.54
Vector Field	0.65	0.14	0.38	0.53

response has a q effort and r effort significantly higher than the others, which can be explained by its high proportional gains.

5.2 Simulations with Wind Disturbances

The path-following algorithms can have different performances when submitted to disturbed environments. Thus, to effectively compare the 3D extended path-following algorithms, a comparison with wind disturbances was also executed, using the kinematic modelling defined in (6)–(10).

For this comparison, it was generated 500 experiments for winds with different intensities and directions, that changed every 1 min. Then, the trajectory described by the waypoints $W_0 = [0,0,0]^T$, $W_1 = [0,500,0]^T$, $W_2 = [500,500,500]^T$, $W_3 = [500,0,500]^T$ and $W_4 = [0,0,0]^T$ was executed by each 3D extended path-following algorithm, with the parameters from Table 3. The initial position of the aircraft for the experiments was $p = [5,30,20]^T$ with $\theta = 0$, $\psi = 0$ and constant velocity of $v = 15\,\text{m/s}$.

The average of the normalised error RMS, normalised effort for q, normalised effort for r and metric were calculated from the trajectories resulting from the 500 experiments for each algorithm. Also, an confidence interval was determined with a 95% confidence level to compare the trajectories [6].

Figure 4 shows the results for the normalised error RMS. It is possible to observe that NLGL_+ has the worst error, while Lookahead has an intermediate value and PLOS and Vector Field have lower errors. This result contrasts with the ones from the simulation without wind, demonstrating the different performance in a disturbed environment.

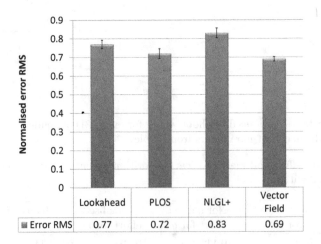

Fig. 4. Average of the normalised error RMS for the 500 experiments with wind disturbances to compare the 3D extended path-following algorithms.

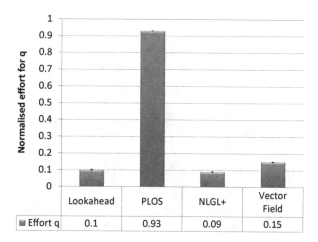

Fig. 5. Average of the normalised effort for q for the 500 experiments with wind disturbances to compare the 3D extended path-following algorithms.

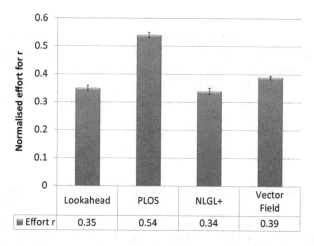

Fig. 6. Average of the normalised effort for r for the 500 experiments with wind disturbances to compare the 3D extended path-following algorithms.

According to the q effort, represented in Fig. 5, the performance is similar to Lookahead, NLGL$_+$ and Vector Field and significantly worse for PLOS, as happened with the simulation without wind. This result was expected because the wind has only yaw direction, influencing very little in the trajectories altitude.

Figure 6 presents the normalised effort for r. The effort is lower for Lookahead and NLGL$_+$, slightly higher for Vector Field and considerably higher for PLOS. The efforts are also similar to the simulation without wind, which indicates that the average eliminates the wind influence in the efforts.

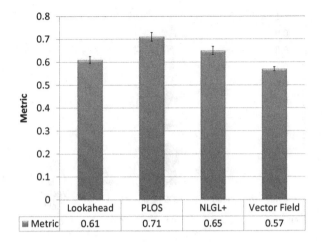

Fig. 7. Average of the metric M for the 500 experiments with wind disturbances to compare the 3D extended path-following algorithms.

The metric, depicted in Fig. 7, shows a better performance for the Vector Field, followed by Lookahead, NLGL$_+$ and, with the worse performance, PLOS. The result is consistent with the simulation without wind and evinces the Vector Field preeminence, as also shown on comparisons in the literature for the 2D scenario [13]. Moreover, PLOS had the worse performance for the 3D scenario, as a consequence of its high effort.

6   Conclusions

The main purpose of this paper is to present new 3D extended path-following algorithms, based in the algorithms Lookahead, NLGL, PLOS and Vector Field. The extension process, which can also be applied to others path-following algorithms, was detailed and a GA method was used to optimise the new algorithms parameters.

The analysis of the new algorithms was performed as a comparison in two different environments. The first environment was the kinematic modelling of an UAV with constant velocity without wind disturbances, in which Vector Field had the best performance and PLOS had the worse one.

In the second environment, winds with different intensities and directions were replicated and applied to the execution of the 3D extended path-following algorithms. The trajectories resulted also elucidated the superiority of Vector Field, with the lowest error and aircraft effort. PLOS had the second lowest error, however, its demanded effort was too high, which affected its performance when compared to the others algorithms. Summarising, NLGL$_+$ and Lookahead had a similar intermediate performance with an effort proportional to Vector Field.

The resulting path-following algorithms can be readily used for UAVs, encompassing their complete movement in the 3D scenarios. Therefore, as future work, it is possible to analyse the new path-following algorithms in a simulation that also considers the dynamic modelling for UAVs and to evaluate their efficiency in experimental flights.

Acknowledgments. The authors acknowledge the support granted by FAPESP through processes 2012/13641-1 and 2015/21249-2.

References

1. Austin, R.: Unmanned Aircraft Systems: UAVS Design, Development and Deployment. Aerospace Series. Wiley, New York (2010)
2. Breivik, M., Fossen, T.I.: Principles of guidance-based path following in 2D and 3D. In: Proceedings of 44th IEEE Conference on Decision and Control, pp. 627–634 (2005). doi:10.1109/CDC.2005.1582226
3. Curry, R., Lizarraga, M., Mairs, B., Elkaim, G.: L+2, an improved line of sight guidance law for UAVs. In: American Control Conference (ACC), pp. 1–6 (2013). doi:10.1109/ACC.2013.6579804
4. Elkaim, G.H., Lie, F.A.P., Gebre-Egziabher, D.: Principles of guidance, navigation, and control of UAVs. In: Valavanis, K.P., Vachtsevanos, G.J. (eds.) Handbook of Unmanned Aerial Vehicles, pp. 347–380. Springer, Dordrecht (2015). doi:10.1007/978-90-481-9707-1_56
5. Gudi, R., Ramana, M., Varma, S.A., Kothari, M.: 4th IFAC conference on advances in control and optimization of dynamical systems acods 2016 motion planning for a fixed-wing UAV in urban environments. IFAC-PapersOnLine **49**(1), 419–424 (2016). doi:10.1016/j.ifacol.2016.03.090
6. Jain, R.: The Art of Computer Systems Performance Analysis: Techniques for Experimental Design, Measurement, Simulation, and Modeling. Wiley Professional Computing. Wiley, Hoboken (1991)
7. Jung, W., Lim, S., Lee, D., Bang, H.: Unmanned aircraft vector field path following with arrival angle control. J. Intell. Robot. Syst. 1–15 (2016). doi:10.1007/s10846-016-0332-5
8. Mathisen, S.H., Gryte, K., Fossen, T.I., Johansen, T.A.: Non-linear model predictive control for longitudinal and lateral guidance of a small fixed-wing UAV in precision deep stall landing. In: AIAA Infotech@ Aerospace, p. 0512 (2016)
9. Mitchell, M.: An Introduction to Genetic Algorithms. MIT Press, Cambridge (1998)
10. Nelson, D., Barber, D., McLain, T., Beard, R.: Vector field path following for miniature air vehicles. IEEE Trans. Robot. **23**(3), 519–529 (2007). doi:10.1109/TRO.2007.898976
11. Park, S., Deyst, J., How, J.P.: Performance and Lyapunov stability of a nonlinear path following guidance method. J. Guid. Control Dyn. **30**(6), 1718–1728 (2007). doi:10.2514/1.28957
12. Pelizer, G.V., Silva, N.B.F., Branco, K.: Um algoritmo de navegação linear 3D para veículos aéreos não tripulados. In: Anais do IV Workshop de Comunicao de Sistemas Embarcados Críticos, pp. 67–75 (2016)

13. Sujit, P., Saripalli, S., Borges Sousa, J.: Unmanned aerial vehicle path following: a survey and analysis of algorithms for fixed-wing unmanned aerial vehicles. IEEE Control Syst. **34**(1), 42–59 (2014). doi:10.1109/MCS.2013.2287568
14. Sujit, P., Saripalli, S., Sousa, J.: An evaluation of UAV path following algorithms. In: European Control Conference (ECC), pp. 3332–3337 (2013)
15. Titterton, D., Weston, J.: Strapdown Inertial Navigation Technology, 2nd edn. Institution of Engineering and Technology (2004)
16. Venkatraman, K., Mani, V., Kothari, M., Postlethwaite, I., Gu, D.W.: A suboptimal path planning algorithm using rapidly-exploring random trees. Int. J. Aerosp. Innov. **2**(1–2), 93–104 (2010)
17. Yamasaki, T., Balakrishnan, S., Takano, H.: Integrated guidance and autopilot for a path-following UAV via high-order sliding modes. In: Proceedings of American Control Conference, pp. 143–148 (2012)
18. Zhang, C., Kovacs, J.M.: The application of small unmanned aerial systems for precision agriculture: a review. Precis. Agric. **13**(6), 693–712 (2012). doi:10.1007/s11119-012-9274-5

An Architecture for Information Fusion and for Detection, Identification and Treatment of Outliers in Wireless Sensor Networks

Patricia Bordignon André[1], Aujor Tadeu C. Andrade[1,2](✉), Rafael Callegaro[3], Carlos Montez[1], Ricardo Moraes[1], and Alex Pinto[1]

[1] Federal University of Santa Catarina, Florianópolis, Brazil
patricia.bordignon@posgrad.ufsc.br,
{carlos.montez,ricardo.moraes,a.r.pinto}@ufsc.br
[2] Federal Institute Catarinense, Florianópolis, Brazil
tadeu@ifc-camboriu.edu.br
[3] Catarinense Water and Sanitation Company, Florianópolis, Brazil
rafael@casan.com.br

Abstract. The fields of precision agriculture, environmental engineering, among others, often have applications that use sensors to monitor the environment. Examples of such applications include pest control, irrigation process, soil fertility mapping, monitoring of forest areas and of urban rivers etc. Wireless sensor networks (WSNs) have been proposed as distributed infrastructures for these applications. These networks produce a large volume of data and use low-cost sensors. However, these sensors usually have low-reliability, generating anomalous data (outliers), affecting the final quality of the monitoring. These conditions imply the need to use methods for outlier detection and treatment, allowing the correct operation of the network and increasing the confidence in the monitored data. This article proposes an architecture for information fusion focusing on low-reliability sensors. The architecture is integrated with techniques for detection and treatment of outliers, and it was evaluated through two case studies. The first one involving low-cost barometric pressure sensors, whose monitored data were processed by outlier detection techniques. The second one involves the LUCE (Lausanne Urban Canopy Experiment) large-scale scenario, whose database is fed by 84 sensors for monitoring weather conditions. The results show that some of the low-level fusion methods and outliers detection techniques, when combined and organized according to the proposed architecture, can replace a single centralized, high-cost sensor, maintaining the confidence of the monitored data.

Keywords: Information fusion · Data fusion · Outlier detection · WSN · Wireless sensor network

1 Introduction

A Wireless Sensor Network (WSN) consists of a network composed of low-cost nodes, with small dimensions and with some processing and transmission

K. Branco et al. (Eds.): WoCCES 2013-2016, CCIS 702, pp. 81–100, 2017.
DOI: 10.1007/978-3-319-61403-8_5

capacity. In this type of network, nodes are equipped with sensors capable of monitoring scalars, and they have capabilities that go beyond of simply collecting information. They have features that allow them to analyze data, remove spurious data, detect events in the environment and perform data fusion of the sensor data, in order to reduce the amount of transmitted data. Usually, nodes communicate with a base station, thus data can be analyzed and eventually stored [1]. The application fields of these networks range from industrial, domestic, military, urban and rural areas [2].

WSNs are becoming widely used in automation monitoring processes of various physical phenomena. One advantages these networks is that they replace traditional centralized monitoring applications, where there is a single sensor monitoring the environment. This sensor, being unique, needs to be highly reliable, robust and expensive. The deployment of this sensor, in order to guarantee the measurements reliability, has a high cost associated. This centralized approach also entails costly maintenance because, commonly, data storage is done in data loggers that are dedicated devices for locally storing data collected by sensors. The high cost of maintenance is also a problem, since there is often a requirement that this type of sensor is deployed in places of difficult access, making it impossible to constantly replace its batteries and making difficult the access to data loggers.

Consequently, several applications that use a WSN infrastructure, such as environmental monitoring, are no longer exclusively investigated by the academy and are gradually being adopted by companies, replacing traditional solutions [3]. However, there are several challenges that need to be overcome, for example: (i) large amount of data, (ii) energy consumption of nodes must be reduced and (iii) there are difficulties in detecting anomalous data, and when these data are detected, they need to classify whether they are spurious data (e.g. resulting from sensor failures) or relevant events in the environment (e.g. forest fire).

This work focuses on problems (i) to (iii), dealing with them from the point of view of data fusion methods [4–7]. These techniques, through the mathematical manipulation of the monitored data set, are capable of handling large amounts of data and can reduce the energy consumption. Besides, they are able to increase the degree of truthfulness of the monitored network data. More specifically, this paper proposes that these problems can be treated in a systematic way, through an information fusion architecture that organizes data flow and the various activities required to integrate different types of data fusion techniques.

The main question that motivates this work is to know if a set of low-cost sensors can replace the conventional use of centralized and high-cost sensors, maintaining, or even increasing, the degree of truthfulness achieved in the monitored data. In the following of this article, the relevant aspects of information fusion are presented in Sect. 2. The proposal of an architecture for the data fusion of WSN low-cost sensor data is presented in Sect. 3. In Sect. 4, a case study is described, which uses low-cost barometric sensors. In Sect. 5, in order to assess the proposed architecture in an environment with a higher number of nodes and greater information traffic, is introduced a case study of temperature sensors installed in a large scale area. Finally, some final considerations and future works are presented.

2 Background

2.1 Information Fusion

Information Fusion (or data fusion) is a largely used denomination [3], and can be defined as the investigation of efficient methods that automatically or semi-automatically can transform information of several sources and with different time stamps to a consistent information. This information can be used by humans or machines for decision making. The advantages of using a multisensor information fusion are high availability, better spatial and temporal coverage and better accuracy and/or precision. However, when a large number of sensors present erroneous sensing values, the global performance of the system can be affected [8,9].

Large WSNs based on low-cost nodes are generally used in the monitoring of scalars. However, these low-cost sensors are not reliable individually. Thus, data fusion methods are used to overcome this low reliability based on the fusion of several sensor readings. This way, data fusion can be used to detect outliers [10].

The techniques for information fusion can be classified according to the abstraction level of the sensed data [11]. In low-level data fusion, the raw sensed data is provided as inputs and combined directly with other raw data, assuming that the resulting data will present more accuracy than the individual inputs. In the intermediate level, the data abstraction occurs in such a way that it is possible to represent an object in a precise and concise way. In the high-level data fusion or decision-making process, decision-making takes place based on information from the low- and middle-level layers, where a priori knowledge and specific information about decision-making can be incorporated.

Data Fusion can be also classified based on the topology of sensors [12]. In the complementary configuration, sensors do not depend directly on each other but act in a cooperative way to obtain a complete picture of the observed phenomenon. In a redundant configuration, independent measurements of the same property are provided at different times or by two or more sources at the same instant in order to provide better accuracy. In the cooperative configuration, information is provided by more than one sensor to derive information that would not be available if only one were used. Typically, in this type of data fusion, there is a loss of precision and reliability.

2.2 Outlier Detection Methods

This section addresses some statistical methods for outlier detection in wireless sensor networks. The choice of these methods is justified: it does not require a history of the previous messages and the low computational nodes consumption.

Detection can be performed, for example, by simple inspection of the sensor operating range. Therefore, the sensed data that are outside the sensor operational range must be discarded.

In outlier data fusion methods, the data of the sensors are compared in order to detect possible conflicting sensors. Several data fusion algorithms can be considered. In our architecture, we consider as an appropriate algorithm, the one with the ability to compare the data obtained by the sensors involved in the data fusion and, following a specific criterion, to decide whether or not to suppress its data. However, it is not desirable to unnecessarily exclude sensor observations when the readings are correct.

Besides, it is convenient that when an observation is discarded, somehow the algorithm has the ability to clearly mark or show which sensor and why the data must discarded. Due to uncertainty about the quality of the low-cost sensors, it is desirable that the algorithm has mechanisms capable of computing sensor quality during the data fusion process.

A widely used method for data fusion is a simple average, which is not suitable for the vast majority of applications. The following subsections describe the main characteristics of methods evaluated in this article. It is important to note that there are several other techniques that could be evaluated, such as, for example, techniques based on the Kalman filter [8]. However, these approaches are statefull, since they require a history of the previous messages of each sensor, and the methods studied in this paper are stateless.

A. Fault Tolerant Average - FTA
One of the methods of sensor fusion with a simple application and good results is the Fault Tolerant Average (FTA) proposed by [13]. Basically, it divides an ordered set of data into three parts, eliminating the edges.

The first step in this technique is to sort the set of data sent by the sensor nodes. Taking $t = N/3$, where N is the size of the set, we discard the borders of the ordered sample, that is, the largest and the smallest t values. This approach assumes that if there are outliers, they will be removed along with those "extreme" values. The final value is the calculation of mean and standard deviation of the remaining values.

B. Confidence-Weighted Averaging - CWA
Elmenreich [3] proposed a data fusion method setting for each sensor a value of "confidence" inversely associated with the variance of the sensor. Variance is a useful measure in many cases because they are additive, thus different groups of data can be compared. The standard deviation, in turn, has the advantage of being expressed in the same unit as the measured variable, making it easier to compare results. Following this approach, in the best case, the variance is close to zero, achieving a maximum confidence value. The worst-case variance can be calculated as the variation of a random function evenly distributed between the limits a and b, where these values are the minimum and maximum values of a uniformly distributed random function.

C. CWA+FTA Method

Elmenreich [3] suggested that CWA could be used in conjunction with other methods, such as FTA proposed by [13]. Thus the method becomes fault tolerant and considers the quality of the sensor in the data fusion. The method consists of calculating the weighted mean including all sensors using the CWA method and subsequently eliminating 2/3 of the sensors as specified in the FTA and calculating the weighted average again.

D. Modified CWA with a Test of Fixed Value Locked Sensor

The method proposed in [3] to fuse information from different sensors, prioritizes the sensors with lower variance. An exception pointed out by the author of the algorithm is that, if the variance is zero, some treatment to avoid division by zero is required. However, in preliminary experiments carried out in this work, another problem was observed, since, as the proposed architecture is focused on WSNs using low-cost sensors. It was observed in some execution scenarios that readings of data collected by a single sensor could have equal values for a long period of time, characterizing a faulty and locked sensor.

This sensor lock may be permanent or temporary for a short or long time. This locked sensor, due to its low variance, makes its incorrect data contribute to a greater weight in the calculation of the weighted average than the correct sensors. Thus, a simple alteration of the original algorithm was necessary for implementation.

Basically, when a sensor exhibits variations between readings below and a specified value (and dependent on the type and specification of the sensor), its calculated variance will be artificially increased to the maximum possible value, thus contributing minimally to the weighted average calculation.

E. Chauvenet Method

The Chauvenet criterion is a statistical method that was developed for detection of outliers, and can be used to Byzantine fault detection. It is based on the hypothesis that an arbitrary measurement can be rejected if the probability of obtaining the deviation from the mean to this value is less than the inverse of twice the number of measurements [14].

The sample size is very important in using the method because, with a large sample, there is little chance that one of the values influence the average significantly. A divergent value in a large sample should be very far from the average to move to distribution. This makes the use of few data requirements.

F. Peirce Criterion

The Peirce method is a statistical technique for detecting outliers, in a sample with normal behavior. The original article dates from 1852, however, it is widely used on current days [14]. The basic idea of the proposed method is that the observations should be rejected when the actual deviations from the mean obtained by keeping them, are less than the deviations obtained by its rejection, multiplied by the probability of making as many and not more, unusual observations. Hence, the goal of his technique was to generate error probabilities occurring in the system where all n observations are retained versus the rejected samples.

Thus, k observations are rejected and it checks whether the sample is closer to normal than previous one. The Peirce Criterion provides for detection of more than one discordant data in the sample. However, Peirce's calculation method is mathematically complex to use. In this way, there are tables derived from the work of Peirce [15] that can be used To improve the performance of the calculations.

3   Architecture for Low-Cost Sensor Data Fusion

In this paper we propose an architecture for monitoring with WSN and divides the activities carried out into three layers: Local Fusion Layer, Low-Level Fusion Layer, Management Layer and User Interface (Fig. 1).

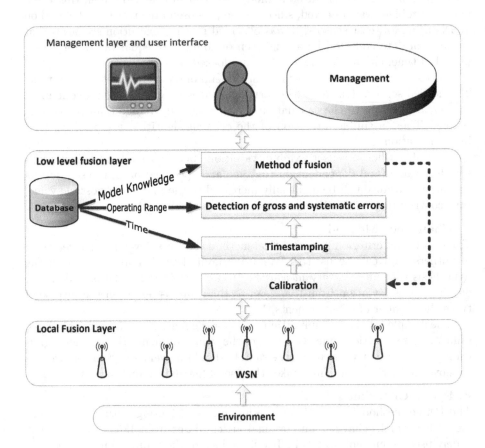

Fig. 1. Proposed architecture for sensor data fusion in WSN.

The main contribution of this article is in the definition of the Low-Level Fusion Layer, which is responsible for receiving data from the WSN, processing, and forwarding to the Management Layer and User Interface layer [11]. Techniques commonly employed in the Local Fusion Layer are presented in the following.

3.1   Local Data Fusion Layer

The purpose of this level of processing is to configure the sensors to collect data about the environment where they are inserted, to perform some type of local data fusion, and to forward the data for the transmission. One of the first steps is to check with the sensor manufacturer the recommended sampling rates.

It is also necessary to check if there is any kind of adjustment to be made in the sensor, such as micro calibration. Depending on the rate, it can be applied locally to the data, such as the arithmetic average. Some methods in the upper layers of the architecture may use other information in its processing, such as variance or variance generated by the local data fusion method. For the calculation of these values, a good option is to perform the fusion between beacons[1].

3.2   The Low-Level Data Fusion Layer

The low-level data fusion layer is subdivided into: calibration; timestamping; detection of systematic and gross errors; methods of fusion and feedback (Fig. 1).

Sensor calibration is a fundamental problem in WSN [16]. It consists of the set of establishes and corrects the difference between a measured value and the true value. In some cases, it may consist of an additive or multiplicative correction of the indication with a measurement uncertainty. As the true value is ignored, the calibration tends to minimize the difference between the read value and the true value of importance.

The calibration of each device, individually and manually, known as a micro-calibration may be intractable when a large number of sensors is considered [16]. Therefore, self-calibration can be employed in this process. A conventional calibration is the readings corrections of each sensor based on a common reference, or be based on the reference of a sensors group [17].

In the proposed architecture, low-level data fusion can be executed online or offline. In the case of off-line data fusion, cluster heads do not perform the role of fusion centers, they only forward the data received towards the PAN coordinator, where the data fusion will be carried out. Offline data fusion can be considered for further study of the observed environment. In this case, it is necessary to associate time stamps referring to the moment of observation of each stored data.

Data Fusion Centers play an important role in the Low-level Data Fusion when online data fusion occur, being paramount in WSN that also have actuators, so that their results can be used immediately.

4   Experimental Assessment

The proposed architecture is tested through a case study. An environmental monitoring application based on atmospheric pressure is used to validate the

---

[1] Beacons are control packets periodically generated by the coordinator to synchronize an IEEE 802.15.4 network.

proposal. Atmospheric pressure is important for several applications like meteorology and environmental engineering. Usually, just one sensor (high-quality sensor) is used, however, it is a high-cost sensor.

The chosen place to execute the experiments was near the Hercilio Luz Airport in Florianópolis, SC-Brazil. Figure 2 shows the external reference sensor that was used for comparison (identified in this work as **Vaisala**), this reference sensor is used by the Brazilian Air Force and is located near the end of an airport landing strip, at 5 m high. The distance between the airport sensor (reference sensor) and the site of the experiments is 1300 m. Moreover, aiming the comparison between the low-cost sensor and the reference sensor, another reference sensor was used (identified in this work as internal reference sensor **Young**).

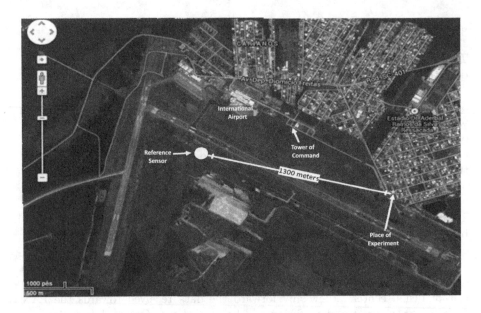

Fig. 2. Place of experiment.

The communication between experimental sensors was performed based on an IEEE 802.15.4 wireless sensor network in star topology. Four low-cost sensors were used in the experiments, which is required by data fusion techniques discussed in previous sessions of this paper.

The fifth node was configured as a PAN coordinator, this node is responsible for storing data. The WSN was configured in beacon mode, PAN coordinator is responsible for synchronizing the networks through beacon sending. In order to configure the network the periodicity of the application was BO =11, that defines a *Beacon Interval* (BI) of 30 s.

Other nodes were equipped with the low-cost sensor, and the system was implemented over the MAC layer. This way, it was not used WSN operating systems like TinyOS or FreeRTOS.

Nodes 1, 2, 3 and 4 use 2 1.5 V batteries for the embedded system and sensors. Node 5 use AC/DC power and was connected to a computer using serial communication. The collected data were stored in text file using the following format: $<timestamp, node[1 - 10]$, variance $[1 - 10]>$.

The base station computer was synchronized through NTP protocol, the same protocol used in the airport system. The data fusion was performed later due to experiment constraints.

4.1   Experimental Results

The first data analysis was based on internal and external reference sensor. The main goal was to verify the proximity of internal and external reference sensors.

It was selected data regarding 24 h of readings and the average of atmospheric pressure was calculated (Fig. 3).

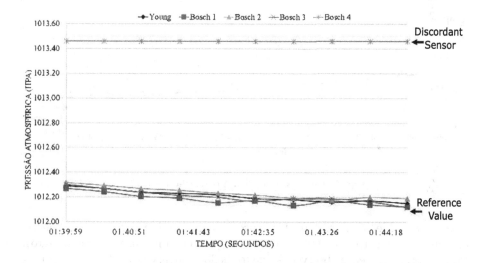

Fig. 3. Reference sensors comparison.

In order to make the comparison, it was necessary to compute the difference of altitude among two sensors (more or less 1.5 m), that is 0.1 hPa. Besides the altitude, it was considered the precision of sensors. It is informed that sensor readings may vary 0,3 hPa, thus the reading difference between two sensors can not be over 0,6 hPa. It was observed that the maximum difference was 0,25 hPa. Thus, we considered that the reference sensor is validated, this validation is based on external reference sensor (Vaisala) that is periodically calibrated, because these readings are used for landing and take-off operations. The data collected by sensors and the results obtained by data fusion will be compared just with the internal reference sensor.

Diverse analysis was performed in order to assess the data fusion techniques. In this paper, we present an analysis of a data sample that contains an incorrect sensor (Fig. 4).

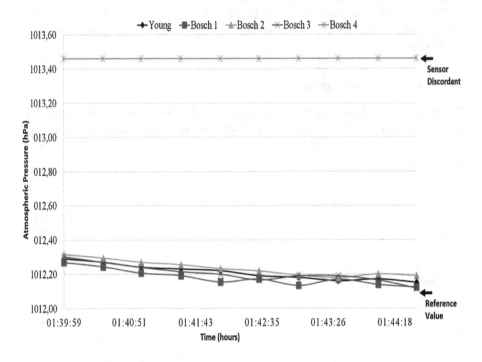

Fig. 4. Data sample with a discordant sensor.

It is possible to note that this sensor always sends the same atmospheric pressure reading, thus it is considered a high precision sensor (variance zero). However, the difference observed is due to the low battery level of nodes. Figure 4 shows that values of Bosch4 sensor remain different from reference sensor 1.31 hPa, and other sensors just 0,07 hPa.

Figure 5 shows the results of data fusion techniques over these data. The average method shows the worst performance due to the fact that all data are considered in the data fusion method. The erroneous sensor in the sample causes a distortion in the final result and it is not possible to detect the outlier. The Chauvenet method detects the sensor 4 as an outlier, obtaining the same result of the arithmetic mean. It is interesting to note that if the reference sensor was considered in data fusion, the Chauvenet method would achieve a better performance: the outlier would be eliminated and the average will be performed with other sensors.

The Peirce method could also detect the sensor 4 as an outlier. The maximum difference between reference sensor and the data fusion value was 0.03 hPa. MTF

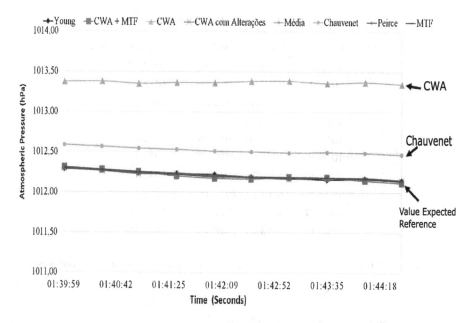

Fig. 5. Application of data fusion methods.

always discard the values of 2/3 of sensors, even if these values are similar, this behavior is not noticed in Chauvenet and Peirce.

Elmenreich method (CWA) can be considered a complete method, because it considers the sensor quality. However, the variance values must be available. There are three ways to execute the method. The first one considers just variance informed by sensors (CWA); the second way includes the modifications proposed in this paper (altered CWA) and, finally, the modified CWA algorithm combined with a fault tolerant average (CWA+FTA).

It is possible to notice that results presented in Table 1 show that Elmenreich method (CWA) presents a bad performance, obtaining a 1,2 hPa from the reference sensor. This result shows that when a sensor presents equal readings, the variance is zero and the system presents the highest level of confidence in the faulty sensor.

When modified CWA method is used, we consider that a sensor with constant variance near zero, during a certain period, is considered an outlier, and its variance is artificially raised to a maximum value. Thus, the use of faulty sensor in the weighted average does not change the result, and an approximate value from the reference sensor was achieved. CWA+MTF achieved values near the reference values.

Table 2 shows the results of MTF and CWA+MTF. It is possible to notice that readings of sensor 2 were considered by all methods and the values from

Table 1. Elmenreich method.

Rounds	Reference	CWA	CWA+FTA	CWA modified
1	1012,29	1013,37	1012,31	1012,30
2	1012,27	1013,38	1012,28	1012,26
3	1012,24	1013,35	1012,25	1012,23
4	1012,23	1013,36	1012,20	1012,23
5	1012,22	1013,36	1012,18	1012,20
6	1012,19	1013,38	1012,17	1012,18
7	1012,18	1013,39	1012,19	1012,17
8	1012,16	1013,36	1012,18	1012,18
9	1012,17	1013,37	1012,15	1012,16
10	1012,15	1013,35	1012,12	1012,15

Table 2. MTF and CWA+MTF averages with sensor 4 as a source of outliers.

	Sensor					Sensor			
	#1	#2	#3	#4		#1	#2	#3	#4
1° round	o	•	•	o	1° round	o	•	•	o
2° round	o	•	•	o	2° round	o	•	•	o
3° round	o	•	•	o	3° round	o	•	•	o
4° round	o	•	•	o	4° round	•	o	•	o
5° round	o	•	•	o	5° round	•	o	•	o
6° round	•	•	o	o	6° round	•	o	•	o
7° round	o	•	•	o	7° round	o	•	•	o
8° round	o	•	•	o	8° round	o	•	•	o
9° round	o	•	•	o	9° round	•	o	•	o
10°round	•	•	o	o	10°round	•	o	•	o
(a) MTF					**(b) CWA with MTF**				

label: • Participates in data fusion   o Does not participate in data fusion

sensor 4 were discarded by CWA+MTF and MTF. However, sensor 1 even presenting correct readings was discarded in 80% of data fusion tasks. When MTF results are compared with reference sensor readings, 0,02 hPa value is showed.

5   Simulation Assessment of a Large-Area WSN

In the previous section, it was concluded that the use of low-cost sensors in a cooperative way to perform the monitoring is equivalent in terms of results to the use of a centralized high-cost sensor. In this section, the goal is to extend the scenario and number of nodes to evaluate the behavior of statistical methods to detect outliers in WSN. Based on this premise and due to the technical difficulties to build a real large-scale WSN, a simulator was used for this study.

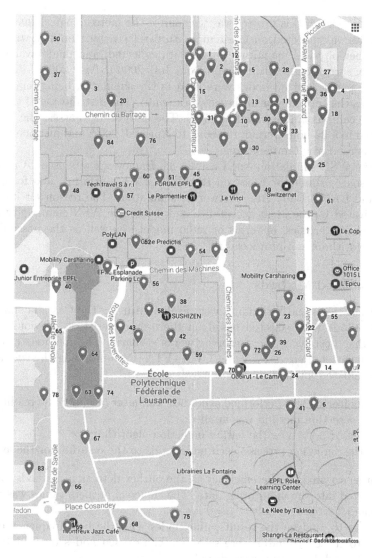

Fig. 6. Sensorscope Lausanne Urban Canopy Experiment (LUCE).

5.1   Large-Area Scenario Description

The dataset used for the simulation and validation of the methods has been obtained through the project LUCE[2] (Lausanne Urban Canopy Experience). The WSN that was structured in a campus of the Federal Polytechnic School of Lausanne (EFPL). This network was deployed with 110 nodes distributed over an area of 300×400 m, characterizing a large-scale WSN [18].

---

[2] http://lcav.epfl.ch/page-86035-en.html.

The objective of this project was to monitor the meteorological changes and various data was collected, such as temperature, relative air humidity, wind speed among other physical magnitudes. The data collected, and made available for public use, corresponds to the period from July 2006 to May 2007.

In this paper, just 85 nodes were used in the simulator, being one of them assumed as the coordinator of the network (sink). The distribution of the nodes across the campus is illustrated in Fig. 6. The data used to assess the methods was sensed in a 24-hour period, referring to April 03, 2007; and just one physical scalar was used: the temperature.

For the WSN simulation, the Castalia 3.0 framework was used[3]. Castalia is an open source simulator based on the OMNeT++ platform[4], and focused on WSNs and BANs (Body Area Networks) simulation. The reason for its choice was motivated by the great acceptance and use in the WSN community for its realistic characteristics, in terms of radio models, as well as the possibility to change algorithms and protocols [19].

5.2   Evaluated Methods

Four outlier statistical techniques were evaluated using the Castalia simulator. These methods were selected based on their characteristics, previously highlighted, that best meet the sensor networks scenario. The methods evaluated were: Chauvenet, Peirce, FTA and CWA+FTA. Parametrizing the simulations for the evaluated methods:

- The monitoring was performed every 30 s and after obtaining 30 readings the outlier detection method was applied;
- Each sensor node uses the outlier detection algorithm;
- After the detection process, each node sends to the coordinator the average.

In order to analyze the efficiency of the outlier detection methods, outliers were inserted into the monitoring data. The choice of outliers values was chosen at random.

In order to analyze the results, nine nodes with the best frequency of submissions to the coordinator were selected. The chosen nodes reached 100% of freight rate and 36 outliers were distributed between nodes.

The Fig. 7 shows the temperature readings of nodes in a fifteen minute period together based on artificial outliers. It is possible to observe the discrepancy of the values and the need for treatment so that these anomalous data do not change the result, thus modifying the real value of the means.

Thus, results for the analyzed methods were described:

- **Chauvenet:** Chauvenet method detected 13 outliers from 36 artificial outliers (Table 3). As can be seen in Fig. 8, points from the temperature of 10 °C, have many points farther from the normal behavior of the captured readings.

---

[3] https://github.com/boulis/Castalia.

[4] https://omnetpp.org/.

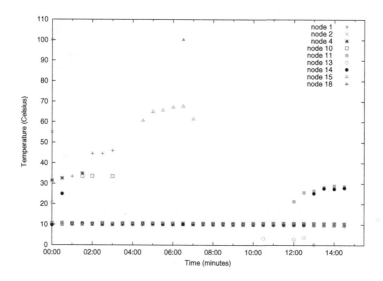

Fig. 7. Sensed values with/without outliers' detection.

- **Peirce:** Peirce technique shows a behavior very similar to that of Chauvenet, 13 outliers were correctly identified (Table 3). In Fig. 9, it is possible to notice that the undiscovered outliers present results very similar to the Chauvenet method.
- **FTA Method:** This method proved to be very efficient in outliers detection, it was able to find all the inserted outliers (Table 3).
  Despite being a relatively simple method it proved to be efficient for detection and removal of outliers. Figure 10 above shows the readings resulting from the FTA method, a problem identified is the aimless removal even of values that are not considered anomalous by always excluding 2/3 of samples.
- **CWA+FTA:** The Elmenreich technique combined with FTA method obtained results similar to the FTA method, reaching 100% efficiency in outliers detection (Table 3).

5.3 Comparative Analysis of Methods

The methods have generally obtained good results in the detection of large-scale WSN outliers. However, the FTA and CWA+FTA methods detected 100% of the outliers. On the other hand, Peirce and Chauvenet methods detected just 36.11% of the outliers. Table 3 shows the outliers detected per node.

The Table 4 presents the final averages of the readings of the nodes by analyzed method. The Table 4 shows the resulting averages. As a result, the table shows that outliers detection techniques are necessary to provide higher accuracy in monitoring. In the analysis, nodes 1, 15 and 18 present high averages, the presence of outliers, which do not correspond to the normal behavior of the

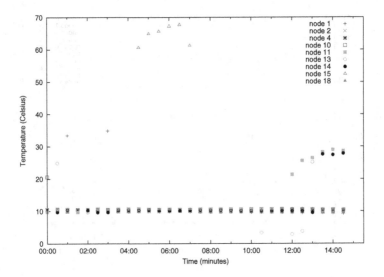

Fig. 8. Event detection using Chauvenet method.

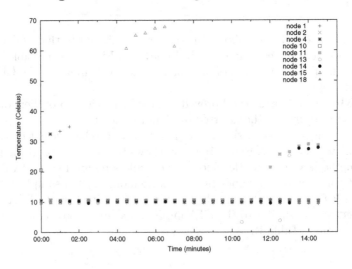

Fig. 9. Event detection using Peirce method.

temperature variation in that period. In this way, it must be withdrawn in order to not disturb the final average.

For example at node 15, six outliers were inserted into the set of readings, which resulted in an average of 20.63 °C degrees. After the application of the CWA+FTA technique, the average resulted in 9.61 °C degrees. Thus, an average reduction in temperature was 46.58% when compared to the average with outliers. FTA technique presented a reduction of 46.97%, while Chauvenet and Peirce techniques did not change the average. Thus, outliers were not removed.

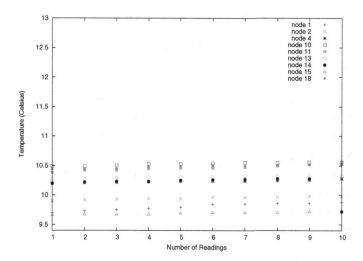

Fig. 10. Event detection using FTA method.

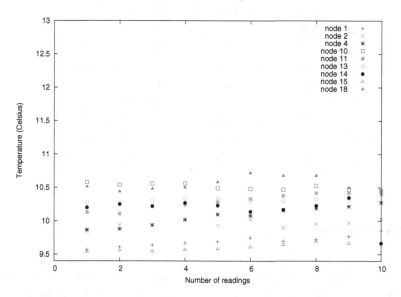

Fig. 11. Result of detection with the CWA+FTA method.

After the detection and removal of the outliers with the FTA and CWA+FTA techniques, it is possible to observe the regularization of final node average, through a data fusion information more accurate and reliable (Fig. 11).

In summary, comparing the outliers detection capability, both the CWA+FTA and the FTA technique achieved the same results, Table 4. Regarding precision, the techniques also obtained similar results, according to Table 4.

Table 3. Amount of outliers detected.

	Total per node	CWA+FTA	FTA	Peirce	Chauvenet
Node 1	5	5	5	3	3
Node 2	1	1	1	1	1
Node 4	3	3	3	2	3
Node 10	3	3	3	3	3
Node 11	6	6	6	0	0
Node 13	4	4	4	2	1
Node 14	6	6	6	0	0
Node 15	6	6	6	0	0
Node 18	2	2	2	2	2
Total	36	36	36	13	13

Table 4. Local averages obtained by each technique, in degrees Celsius.

	Simple average	CWA+FTA	FTA	Peirce	Chauvenet
Node 1	14,86	9,69	9,80	11,51	11,51
Node 2	11,39	9,95	9,94	9,89	9,89
Node 4	12,46	10,07	10,23	10,98	10,18
Node 10	12,81	10,51	10,53	10,51	10,51
Node 11	13,61	10,29	10,46	13,61	13,61
Node 13	9,24	10,30	10,30	9,81	9,56
Node 14	13,27	10,23	10,25	13,27	13,27
Node 15	20,63	9,61	9,69	20,63	20,63
Node 18	16,42	10,54	10,48	10,45	10,45

6   Conclusions

WSNs based on low-cost sensors have been replacing the traditional centralized systems that use a single, reliable, high-cost sensor. WSN advantages like
deployment flexibility, better area coverage and low-cost sensors are the main
reasons for its choose. However, new challenges emerge as these networks become
popular. For example, they generate a large amount of data, need to have an
adequate operation due to its limited energy budget, as well as failures and errors
caused by WSN nodes equipped with low-cost sensors. Thus the use of raw data
generated by sensor nodes has not been suitable.

Therefore, this work focuses on these problems, treating them from the point
of view of the methods of information fusion, that is, techniques that reduce the
amount of data and increase its reliability. The proposed architecture was applied
in the monitoring of environments. Low-cost sensors were calibrated based on
a reference sensor. Without this operation, the fusion methods would not reach

the expected performance due to the constant deviation of the values observed in the low-cost sensors. The timestamps were added, making it feasible to perform offline the data fusion. Systematic and gross errors, such as "zero" values, were correctly discarded before reaching the fusion methods.

Among the experimentally tested methods, Peirce and CWA+FTA were more suitable for the fusion of the sensors. However, the arithmetic means, Chauvenet and CWA without modifications, did not perform well in the presence of faulty nodes.

In the simulation of a large-scale WSN, the CWA+MTF and FTA methods were the best at eliminating all outliers; while the Chauvenet and Peirce methods did not perform satisfactorily since they did not detect much of the outliers. Regarding accuracy, the Chauvenet and Peirce techniques obtained poor results in their means when compared to CWA+FTA and FTA. Therefore, the CWA+FTA and FTA techniques have achieved good results in the large-scale simulated WSN scenarios giving good detection, accuracy and reliability in monitoring.

As a conclusion, the WSN configuration used in conjunction with low-cost sensors and the proposed architecture deliver as good performance as the use of a single high-cost sensor.

Acknowledgement. The authors would like to acknowledge the support from the following funding agencies: CAPES-Brazil and CNPq-Brazil.

References

1. Dargie, W., Poellabauer, C.: Fundamentals of Wireless Sensor Networks: Theory and Practice. Wiley, Hoboken (2010)
2. Akyildiz, I.F., Su, W., Sankarasubramaniam, Y., Cayirci, E.: Wireless sensor networks: a survey. Comput. Netw. **38**(4), 393–422 (2002)
3. Elmenreich, W.: Fusion of continuous-valued sensor measurements using confidence-weighted averaging. J. Vibr. Control (Incorporating Modal Anal.) **13**(9–10), 1303–1312 (2007)
4. Pinto, A.R., Montez, C., Araújo, G., Vasques, F., Portugal, P.: An approach to implement data fusion techniques in wireless sensor networks using genetic machine learning algorithms. Inf. Fusion **15**, 90–101 (2014)
5. Andrade, A., Montez, C., Moraes, R., Pinto, A., Vasques, F., da Silva, G.: Outlier detection using k-means clustering and lightweight methods for wireless sensor networks. In: IECON 2016–42nd Annual Conference of the IEEE Industrial Electronics Society, pp. 4683–4688. IEEE (2016)
6. Budke, G.F., Montez, C., Moraes, R., Portugal, P.: A dynamic communication approach for data fusion in IEEE 802.15.4 wireless sensor networks. In: 2012 IEEE 17th Conference on Emerging Technologies & Factory Automation (ETFA), pp. 1–8. IEEE (2012)
7. Pinto, A., Bitencort, B.R., Correa, U.C., Dantas, M., Montez, C.: Probabilistic real-time data fusion in wireless sensor networks with ZigBee. IFAC Proc. Volumes **40**(22), 267–272 (2007)

8. Nakamura, E.F., Loureiro, A.A.F., Frery, A.C.: Information fusion for wireless sensor networks: methods, models, and classifications. ACM Comput. Surv. **39**(3) (2007)
9. Fawzy, A., Mokhtar, H.M., Hegazy, O.: Outliers detection and classification in wireless sensor networks. Egypt. Inform. J. **14**(2), 157–164 (2013)
10. Zhou, C.-H., Chen, B., Gao, Y., Zhang, C., Guo, Z.-J.: A technique of filtering dirty data based on temporal- spatial correlation in wireless sensor network. Procedia Environ. Sci. **10**, 511–516 (2011)
11. Dasarathy, B.: Sensor fusion potential exploitation-innovative architectures and illustrative applications. Proc. IEEE **85**(1), 24–38 (1997)
12. Durrant-Whyte, H.F.: Sensor models and multisensor integration. Int. J. Rob. Res. **7**(6), 97–113 (1988)
13. Marzullo, K.: Tolerating failures of continuous-valued sensors. ACM Trans. Comput. Syst. **8**(4), 284–304 (1990)
14. Ross, S.: Peirce's criterion for the elimination of suspect experimental data. J. Eng. Technol. **20**(2) (2003)
15. Gould, B.A.: On peirce's criterion for the rejection of doubtful observations, with tables for facilitating its application. Astron. J. **4**, 81–87 (1855)
16. Tan, R., Xing, G., Yuan, Z., Liu, X., Yao, J.: System-level calibration for data fusion in wireless sensor networks. ACM Trans. Sen. Netw. **9**(3), 28:1–28:27 (2013)
17. Bychkovskiy, V., Megerian, S., Estrin, D., Potkonjak, M.: A collaborative approach to in-place sensor calibration. In: Zhao, F., Guibas, L. (eds.) IPSN 2003. LNCS, vol. 2634, pp. 301–316. Springer, Heidelberg (2003). doi:10.1007/3-540-36978-3_20
18. Ingelrest, F., Barrenetxea, G., Schaefer, G., Vetterli, M., Couach, O., Parlange, M.: SensorScope. ACM Trans. Sens. Netw. **6**(2), 1–32 (2010)
19. Boulis, A.: Castalia A simulator for Wireless Sensor Networks and Body Area Networks - User's Manual Version 3.0, no. March, p. 79 (2010). http://castalia.npc.nicta.com.au/pdfs/Castalia - User Manual.pdf

A P2P Network for Multimedia Content Sharing Using Android-Based Mobile Devices

Mario M. Teixeira[1,2](✉), Felipe A.O. Machado[2], and Adriano V. Pinto[1,2]

[1] Graduate Program in Computer Science (PPGCC), Federal University of Maranhão (UFMA), São Luís, MA 65080-805, Brazil
mario@deinf.ufma.br

[2] Laboratory of Advanced Web Systems (LAWS), Informatics Department (DEINF), UFMA, São Luís, Brazil

Abstract. Traditionally, P2P networks have used common computers, but more recently, with the widespread use of mobile devices, we note the growing trend of convergence of technologies in these devices, which should be accompanied by P2P networks. This article specifies and implements a P2P network architecture based on mobile devices running on the Android platform. It also developed an application for sharing multimedia content via streaming over this P2P network. The results obtained were very encouraging and support further investigation. Performance tests have shown that connection speed and video coding rate were determinant factors on response time and system throughput, and CPU utilization was also moderate varying from 20 to 50% in most cases observed.

Keywords: Android · Mobile devices · Multimedia · Peer-to-peer

1 Introduction

Peer-to-Peer (P2P) networks have been in the everyday lives of many people for more than a decade. They arose initially with the aim of sharing content between users without the need of a central server, as in the case of the client-server paradigm. P2P networks rapidly evolved towards sharing of entertainment-related content such as music, video, games, etc., often associated with piracy, since many users shared and still share the files stored on their disks without proper attention to copyright issues. In order to share files, famous architectures such as Napster, Gnutella and Kazaa appeared.

Another use of P2P networks is by exploiting idle CPU cycles of the equipments connected to the network, which are then used as nodes of a virtual parallel machine, distributed throughout the network, as in the case of the SETI@HOME project. Additionally, P2P networks can be used to deliver multimedia services, such as streaming audio and video, either on demand or in real time, such as in the case of Skype and Content Distribution Networks (CDNs) such as Akamai.

© Springer International Publishing AG 2017
K. Branco et al. (Eds.): WoCCES 2013-2016, CCIS 702, pp. 101–116, 2017.
DOI: 10.1007/978-3-319-61403-8_6

For a long time, most of the P2P network nodes were just desktop personal computers or notebooks. Currently, with the popularization of smartphones, tablets and mobile devices in general, with ever increasing processing power, more and more P2P networks are being used from mobile platforms. However, what is observed is that these devices usually act only as clients of the network, simply consuming resources, without sharing their stored content or providing any kind of services to their peers.

In particular, the use of P2P networks for streaming media services has received considerable attention from researchers in the field, as it allows the devices to function as a distributed storage medium, contributing, seeking and obtaining multimedia content autonomously [8]. Differently from traditional client/server computing, the peer-to-peer paradigm allows direct collaboration between users, without relying on centralized servers administered by third parties (Rocha et al., 2004).

As for the development of mobile applications, the Android platform has been receiving a lot of acceptance by the developer community because it is an open source initiative available to the general public, it has extensive documentation and it demands a relatively low upfront investment in hardware. Furthermore, it presents a soft learning curve for the creation of applications, by using the popular Java programming language, in addition to a very extensive user base with great growth potential, reasons that make this platform highly attractive to developers and users.

This article proposes and implements a peer-to-peer network architecture, called P2PDroid, aimed at sharing multimedia content between mobile devices interconnected by a P2P network. It also describes a prototype of this network, implemented in devices based on the Android operating system. Moreover, It features an application built on top of the P2PDroid architecture, called *Playinbuddy*, which automatically and transparently allows the sharing of multimedia content by streaming between the various nodes of the P2PDroid network. Finally, a performance evaluation of the presented solution was done, which demonstrated the feasibility of the architecture proposed here.

The P2PDroid architecture allows the formation of ad hoc networks in an uncomplicated way between mobile devices close to each other, without the need for them to be connected to an infra-structured Wi-Fi network or even to hold a valid IP address. As possible scenarios, a P2P network with entertainment purposes could be formed between nearby mobile devices on a sports arena (or in a food court) with the intent of distributing audio and video on demand between smartphones using the Playinbuddy app. Similar uses could be found on a industrial plant or in the countryside, e.g., for the dissemination of sensor-captured data between nearby cell phones, without the need of a possibly unreachable central server.

In the current stage of this work, a P2PDroid network prototype was implemented using the Wi-Fi Direct standard, using the UPnP protocol for multimedia content delivery. However, this architecture is not tied to any specific underlying protocol and can be ported to different systems.

The remainder of this article is organized as follows: Sect. 2 describes related work to this proposal. Section 3 briefly discusses the architecture of the Android operating system and applications. Section 4 presents the Wi-Fi Direct standard used in the implementation of the P2PDroid network prototype, which is detailed in Sect. 5. Section 6 describes the PlayinBuddy application and Sect. 7 presents a few performance evaluation results. Finally, Sect. 8 discusses conclusions and future work.

2 Related Work

A few solutions that allow streaming of multimedia content between mobile devices in domestic ad hoc networks are found in the market. AirServer [1] is a proprietary solution consisting of an Airplay receiver (proprietary protocol developed by Apple) and the application allows users to send media streams from their iOS devices to Mac computers. As an example scenario, it allows a teacher to broadcast a presentation from his iPad to a MacBook connected to a projector. You can also make any game developed to the iOS operating system become multiplayer with up to 16 simultaneous connections. AirServer is compatible with several third-party applications such as YouTube, Vevo, and Air Media Center and is a powerful multimedia content sharing tool for domestic networks, provided that all devices are manufactured by Apple or compatible with its protocols, which dramatically reduces the interoperability of this solution, and make it too expensive for a certain user profile.

Bubble UPnP Server [3] is a multimedia content server that uses the UPnP protocol and also provides an application for devices running Android that allows a smartphone to be able to connect to the server and play multimedia content in real time. It can run on any platform with Java 1.6 or higher, including multiple versions of Windows, MacOS X and Linux. However, the installation and configuration of this solution is not automatic and can be somewhat cumbersome for lay users. However, mobile devices can play only the role of multimedia content receivers, not providers.

Another noteworthy solution is the PS3 Media Server, a UPnP media server compatible with DLNA [4]. Written in Java, it supports all major operating systems, with versions for Windows, Linux and MacOS X. Using this solution, you can stream, transcode and receive multimedia content directly from the Playstation 3 console or Xbox 360, with little or no configuration. It offers a user-friendly and intuitive user interface, as well as support for a wide range of media content formats.

As can be seen, the majority of solutions found tend to require proprietary software or hardware, making them more expensive. Most of them only allow stream transmission in only one direction (server to client), in addition to having a central point or hub, which is at least used for initial setup purposes. On the other hand, the P2PDroid network presented in this article has automatic and immediate configuration and, as we shall demonstrate in the remainder of this paper, does not require a central server and allows each device to play the role of either server or client as needed. Moreover, the P2PDroid network runs on the Android operating system, the most popular platform for mobile devices nowadays, endorsed by a wide range of manufacturers and appealing to several types of users and purposes.

3   Android Platform

Android is a software platform maintained by Google and the Open Handset Alliance [6] that has revolutionized the global mobile phone market.

The architecture of the Android operating system is divided into layers (Fig. 1), with the Linux Kernel as the basic supporting layer, allowing an abstraction between hardware and software. It is also responsible for crucial services in any operating system, such as memory management and process scheduling.

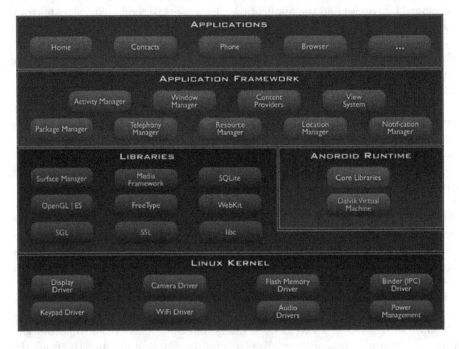

Fig. 1. Android architecture (Source: [2]).

The top layer, the Application layer, is composed of software such as internet browsers, e-mail clients, maps, games and third-party applications, all written using the Java programming language and exploiting application frameworks of the second layer related to file access, telephony, location information, notifications, alarms, etc.

These frameworks use C/C++ libraries provided by the next layer. They allow the developer to have access to system resources such as SQLite database, OpenGL 3D graphics API, media libraries, a surface manager, and so on.

Applications on Android OS, although written in Java, do not run on a conventional Java Virtual Machine (JVM), but rather on the Dalvik virtual machine, native to Android. Dalvik VM is a register-based virtual machine, optimized for low memory devices and designed so that multiple instances can be run simultaneously. The operating system is responsible for process scheduling, thread support and memory management services. Dalvik also implements its own class library, and it is not fully compliant with J2SE or J2ME specifications.

Unlike the conventional JVM from Oracle, Dalvik does not run Java byte-codes, which are rather converted to .dex (Dalvik Executable) files and compressed into a single .apk extension package (Android Package), which is how Android applications are distributed. Android applications fall into four basic blocks: Activities, Services, Content Providers and Broadcast Receivers. An Activity is an application component that provides a screen users can interact with (the GUI, so to speak). A typical Android application usually consists of several Activities.

A Service is an application component that can perform long-running operations in the background and does not have a user interface. An application should bind to a service using traditional interprocess communication before any interaction between them is initiated.

Content Providers manage access to a set of structured data, encapsulating them and providing mechanisms for data security. A content provider connects a dataset with code running in another process. For instance, if the developer needs to access phone contacts, it can do so through its specific Content Provider.

Finally, Broadcast Receiver is the component that responds to general system alerts, which can be generated by Activities, Services or other modules and captured by applications.

4 Wi-Fi Direct Communication Standard

Wi-Fi Direct (Android Developers, 2013) is a recent technology that allows you to turn any Android device into an access point. It is a new specification created by Wi-Fi Alliance that enables you to create ad hoc networks between Wi-Fi devices with the same ease found in Bluetooth connections. Instead of connecting devices to a central access point, this new protocol transforms any device that has Wi-Fi technology into a potential access point (Fig. 2).

The Wi-Fi Direct standard was the technology chosen to implement communication between devices connected to the P2PDroid network.

4.1 Architecture

In a typical Wi-Fi scenario, customers look for and connect to available wireless networks, which are created and announced by Access Points (AP's). Each of these devices has a different set of features and in Wi-Fi Direct these roles are specified as dynamic, so a Wi-Fi Direct device can implement both the role of

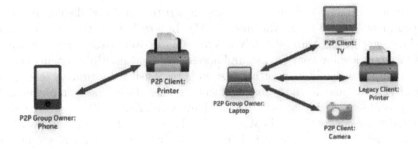

Fig. 2. Wi-Fi direct utilization scenario.

client and of an AP (or server). These roles are logical functions that can even be executed simultaneously by the same device.

Devices implementing Wi-Fi Direct communicate by establishing P2P Groups, which are functionally equivalent to traditional Wi-Fi networks with pre-defined infrastructure. As shown in Fig. 3, the device that becomes the group owner is called P2P Group Owner (P2P GO) while the device acting as a client is known as P2P Client. The assignment of these roles, as already mentioned, is done logically and is dynamic, which makes the architecture quite flexible, as is desirable in a solution for P2P networks.

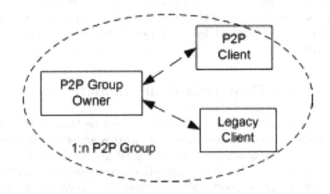

Fig. 3. P2P components and topology of a Wi-Fi direct network.

4.2 Wi-Fi P2P API

Programming applications using Wi-Fi Direct is done through the Wi-Fi P2P API[1] that allows devices running Android 4.0 (API level 14) or higher, with

---

[1] https://developer.android.com/index.html.

appropriate hardware, to connect directly to any other device, via Wi-Fi, without using an access point as an intemediary. Through this API, an application can discover and connect to other devices that support Wi-Fi Direct and then communicate with superior speed and over longer distances than on a Bluetooth connection. This makes Wi-Fi Direct especially useful for applications that share data between users, such as multiplayer games, photo sharing and multimedia applications.

5 P2PDroid Network

As one of the contributions of this paper, this section describes the architecture of a peer-to-peer network for mobile devices based on the Android operating system. The P2PDroid network provides users with a basic infrastructure for communication and sharing of resources. It was implemented using the Wi-Fi P2P Manager API created by Google.

For an Android mobile device to connect to the P2PDroid network, all you have to do is install a small application called P2PDroid Client, designed for Android version 4.0 or higher. It implements the main functionalities of the P2PDroid network and allows communication and transfer of data between different interconnected devices.

5.1 Architecture

The P2PDroid network defines some basic operations, essential for its operation and inspired by the Gnutella P2P network architecture:

- Initialize(): Registers the client application with the Wi-Fi Framework and must be called as soon as the application is started. This registration is required for the application to be able to use the device's Wi-Fi features, such as being notified when Wi-Fi state changes (ON/OFF) or when receiving a connection request from another device.
- DiscoverPeers(): Starts discovering network peers. This operation is used to initiate the discovery of peers (nodes) within the range of the device.
- RequestPeers(): When it detects a device in range (through the DiscoverPeers() operation), it asks each of them to return its own list of visible peers, so that the requesting peer can begin to form its own view of the existing P2P network.
- Connect(): Starts a peer-to-peer connection with a device. Sends an invitation to connect to another device, which can accept or decline the request.
- Disconnect(): Terminates a connection to another device.

Further details about the architecture and operation of the P2PDroid network can be found in [5]. They are omitted here for conciseness.

5.2 P2PDroid Client

Using the Wi-Fi P2P API mentioned above, an application was implemented that facilitates the discovery, connection and exchange of messages between interconnected mobile devices. This architecture works similarly to the Bluetooth standard, so the devices do not need to have an IP address, but peer discovery is limited to the range of the device involved.

In terms of hardware, Wi-Fi Direct works with the device's Wi-Fi. This is an advantage of this architecture when compared to similar ones because it increases the range of peer discovery, file transfer speed and connection stability, being more robust than its competitors (Bluetooth 3.0, for example).

The P2PDroid Client implements the basic operations defined in Sect. 5.1, using the Wi-Fi P2P API that interacts directly with the Wi-Fi Direct standard. At the current stage of development, the client enables automatic network peer discovery and file sharing between nodes. Communication between nodes of the P2PDroid network is performed using the well-known Socket API, which can operate in conventional or secure mode, as reported in (Machado, 2013).

The P2PDroid code was implemented with extensibility in mind, so that one can leverage its infrastructure to develop several types of applications. One of them is described in Sect. 6.

6 Sharing Multimedia Content: PlayinBuddy

In order to illustrate the potential of the P2PDroid network, an application for multimedia content sharing between network nodes has been specified and implemented. It is another main contribution of this work.

This application, called *PlayinBuddy*, is actually a software-defined network of mobile devices that allows streaming of audio and video files between devices connected to the P2PDroid network. It makes possible to listen to or watch multimedia content without having to first download it from its source node. Multimedia content can be accessed at any time by any device without previous configuration and the devices only need to be connected to the P2PDroid network to receive and transmit media streams. Copyright issues were not addressed at this point and are left as future work.

At the current stage, network peers discover and connect through the Wi-Fi P2P API used to deploy the P2PDroid network. For the purposes of multimedia communication itself, a Java program using UPnP [7], defined by DLNA (DLNA, 2013), was implemented through the Cling API. P2PDroid network functions as an overlay for interconnection and exchange of control information between network peers, and multimedia content is then streamed over the UPnP protocol, widely used in home networks.

6.1 Architecture

In the design of the PlayinBuddy application, the following packages have been defined:

- **com.playinbuddy.util** - Encapsulates classes to solve common tasks such as object type conversions, definition and management of application scope variables, callback functions, etc.
- **com.playinbuddy.players** - Encapsulates classes needed to play required media contents (audio and video) on the receiving devices.
- **com.playinbuddy.mediaserver** - Encapsulates classes needed to implement the UPnP media content client-server functions.
- **com.playinbuddy.activities** - Encapsulates classes that manage the application's user interface, in addition to calls to services.
- **com.playinbuddy.objects** - Encapsulates classes that represent objects handled by the application (Device and Media Content).
- **com.playinbuddy.adapters** - Encapsulates classes that work as adapters between the data and views (GridView, ListView and TabView) used.

Figure 4 illustrates a class diagram for the PlayinBuddy application.

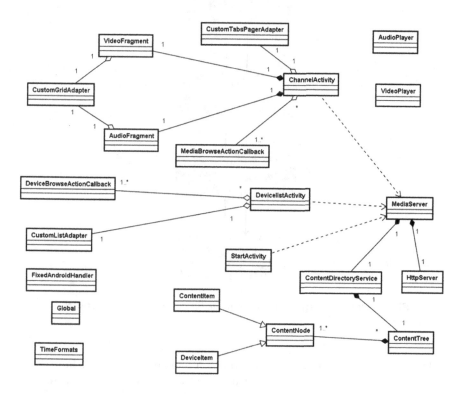

Fig. 4. Class diagram of the PlayinBuddy application.

One of the main classes in the diagram is the MediaServer, which three application activities (user interfaces), namely StartActivity, DevicelistActivity and ChannelActivity depend on. This, in turn, consists of an HTTP server

(HttpServer) and a directory service (ContentDirectoryService). The ContentN-ode class is a generalization of media items that can be found on devices and composes a content tree (ContentTree) used in the directory service. The AudioFragment and VideoFragment classes make up the screen representing the media channel (ChannelActivity), which in turn adds a tabbed display adapter (CustomTabsPagerAdapter) and another class to fill the data in grid views (CustomGridView) on each tab. The purpose of each class will become more evident in Sect. 6.2 which explains the operation of the PlayinBuddy application.

6.2   Application Life Cycle

Playinbuudy can go through different stages in its life cycle, as illustrated in Fig. 5.

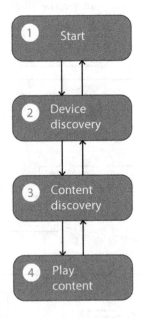

Fig. 5. Operation steps of the multimedia content sharing network.

1. **Start** - The user starts the application on a mobile device, loads information necessary for the operation of sharing services (device addresses, directory service mount, etc.) and waits for user actions through its main screen (Fig. 6).
2. **Device discovery** - The user is informed about which devices (multimedia content transmitters and receivers) are available. The local device also becomes capable of transmitting its multimedia content. A notification message is transmitted to all UPnP devices and services so that they can be identified. Each receiver decides whether it should respond directly (with

UDP datagrams) to the source control point. Figure 7 illustrates the in-app device discovery screen.

3. **Multimedia content discovery** - After selecting a particular device, the user can choose from audio and video items available for playback via streaming. In this step, the directory service is invoked to mount a multimedia content tree on the local device. Figure 8 illustrates the in-app multimedia content discovery screen.

4. **Media content playback** - Finally, using a player suitable to the selected media, the user can either listen to an audio item or watch a video item. Figure 9 illustrates the screen for playing multimedia content in the application.

Fig. 6. PlayinBuddy application splash screen.

6.3   Distinguishing Features

Such an appication actually provides a media streaming service inside a domestic network. Multimedia content can then be accessed by any device any time without prior configuration, i.e., a device just needs to be connected to the home network to receive and transmit media streams.

Network technology used is irrelevant. It does not matter if the mobile device is connected via Wi-Fi, coaxial cable, telephone line, power line or Ethernet cable. Peer-to-peer (decentralized) structure facilitates device interconnection directly without intermediaries and everyone can act both as a Receiver or Provider of multimedia content.

The main limitations of the proposed architecture are:

Fig. 7. Device discovery screen.

Fig. 8. Multimedia content available for streaming.

Fig. 9. Multimedia playback.

- **Data security mechanism** - UPnP protocol specification assumes all necessary security will be provided by other means such as 802.11 WEP, WPA11, NAT12, firewalls and VPNs13. This lack of security requirements specification makes more cautious users disable the UPnP protocol on their devices.
- **Network message overload** - As previously seen, the discovery of new devices or services is based on broadcast messages. Consequently, if several UPnP devices are present on a subnet, a large part of the bandwidth will be occupied by broadcast messages from the devices.

7 Performance Evaluation

This section reports some performance tests performed on the PlayinBuddy network in order to determine its suitability for the transmission of multimedia streams in a mobile environment.

7.1 Experimental Design

As a scenario, it is considered a Motorola mobile phone model Razr i XT890 running Android OS version 4.1.2, and a Samsung Galaxy Tab 2 tablet model GT-P3110 running Android version 4.0.3, both connected to a Wi-Fi network through a Nano Station M5 that allows bandwidth restriction for testing purposes.

As factors that may influence the outcome of the experiment, we considered Video Encoding (Factor A), Connection Speed (Factor B) and Device Type

Table 1. Factorial planning of the experiment (2^3).

Factor	−1	+1
Video encoding	H.264 360p	H.264 720p
Connection speed	Up to 11 Mbps	Up to 300 Mbps
Device type	Smartphone	Tablet

(Factor C). For each factor two levels were defined resulting in an experiment 2^3 as shown in Table 1.

As for video encoding, specifications H.264 360p and H.264 720p were chosen to represent videos with low and high image quality, respectively. Connection speed was defined as an 802.11b network (up to 11 Mbps) for low bandwidth networks and as an 802.11 network (up to 300 Mbps) for high bandwidth. Finally, as device types we picked an smartphone with lower processing capacity and screen resolution and a tablet with higher processing power and screen resolution.

Each experiment was repeated five times and lasted 30 seconds counting from the beginning of content playback. The Playinbuddy application was kept running in the foreground during the whole experiment on each device.

As performance metrics, response time (R), utilization (U), throughput (X) and error rate (E) were used. Response time was defined as the interval between the start of requests and the fulfillment of these requests by the content provider. Throughput rate defines the number of requests per unit of time. Utilization represents processor usage in each device. Finally, error rate was defined as the percentage of packets lost on the network.

Measurements were performed using the Android Debug Bridge utility (ADB), which provides a debug shell for the Android operating system through a USB cable connected to the device or through a TCP/IP port. It allows execution of commands in the background, such as *top* and *vmstat*, while the Playinbuddy app is running on the device's main screen. Data was collected at regular five second intervals. Android keeps performance statistics in system files stored in the */proc* directory, and performance data in */proc/stat*.

7.2   Results and Discussion

This section presents and discusses the most relevant results, as well as the influence of the different factors A, B and C, individually, on the results and also the combination of these on the metrics evaluated, as shown in Table 2.

It is observed that connection speed (B) is the most influential factor in response time, with a percentage of 56.05% and also accounts for an important part of the throughput (variation of 31.39%), together with video encoding (A), with an influence of 27.64%. Joint influence of these two factors (AB) is 26.74% in system throughput. Video encoding has also an important influence on CPU utilization (26.42%), which also shows some dependence on device type (10.71%), especially when considered in conjunction with video encoding (22.73%). Device

Table 2. Influence of factors on application performance.

Parameter	Estimated average				Variation			
	R	X	U	E	R	X	U	E
q0	0,7625	0,8823	30,37	0,006	-	-	-	-
qA	0,9232	1,7523	56,71	0	8,13%	27,64%	26,42%	0%
qB	2,4237	1,8672	20,02	0,1312	56,05%	31,39%	3,29%	42,67%
qC	0,0121	0,0562	36,12	0	0,001%	0,001%	10,71%	0%
qAB	1,6231	1,7234	44,72	0,1102	25,13%	26,74%	16,43%	30,02%
qAC	0,1632	0,2313	52,60	0	0,25%	0,48%	22,73%	0%
qABC	1,0454	1,2341	49,83	0,1052	10,42%	13,71%	20,4%	27,29%

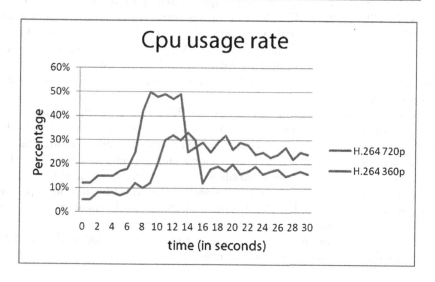

Fig. 10. CPU utilization.

type (C) had little influence on the metrics evaluated when considered individually. The influence of the combination of factors A and B on all response variables (qAB line) is also worthy mentioning. Dependency percentages obtained for error rate (E) do not have much relevance due to the fact that the error measured was actually very small.

A study of the effect of video encoding on network performance was also performed (Fig. 10). It is observed that the maximum CPU utilization reached by the workload (with H.264 720p encoding) is only 50% and stabilizes between 20 to 30%. When H.264 360p encoding is used, utilization reaches 33% and stabilizes between 10 and 20%. Thus CPU utilization in 720p H.264 encoding is on average 50% higher than in Hp64 encoding 360p. It is also possible to infer that the application does not cause overhead in both encodings used. This reinforces our findings on Table 2 where CPU utilization is 30% in average.

Our experiments demonstrated the P2PDroid content sharing network requires a moderate processing power from mobile devices and behaves in a satisfactory manner even when used with high quality videos. Bandwidth levels, however, are important for good application performance. Finally, using smartphones or tablets has little influence P2PDroid performance.

8   Conclusion

This work described a peer-to-peer network architecture, namely *P2PDroid*, specified and implemented on mobile devices based on the Android operating system. This network consists of an abstract specification, inspired by the Gnutella protocol. As proof of concept, we have implemented one P2PDroid version using the Wi-Fi P2P API, by Google, that works with Wi-Fi Direct standard for device interconnection, available for Android 4.0+ devices. As strong points, we highlight non-dependence on infra-structured Wi-Fi for communication between devices, automatic discovery of nearby devices, and maximum speed higher than Bluetooth 3.0, besides being a feasible solution for home entertainment involving games and multimedia.

As a prototype application on top of the P2PDroid network, we developed a multimedia resource sharing application, called *PlayinBuddy*, which uses the UPnP protocol for multimedia content delivery by streaming. Using Playinbuddy, devices can discover each other quickly and instantly and users can play music and watch videos on their handhelds easily, without the need to actually download media. Performance tests have shown that the PlayinBuddy application can run on different handheld types at varying media encoding rates and had only a 50% impact on CPU utilization of the devices involved.

As future work, we intend to implement a version of PlayinBuddy based on the Wi-Fi Direct protocol and develop other types of applications on top of the P2PDroid network.

References

1. AirServer: Dynamic Airserver (2017). https://www.airserver.com/
2. Android Developers: Android architecture (2017). https://developer.android.com/develop/index.html
3. Bubblesoft: Bubblesoft UPnP Server (2017). https://www.bubblesoftapps.com/bubbleupnpserver/
4. DLNA: Digital living network alliance (2017). https://www.dlna.org/
5. Machado, F.A.O.: Aplicações seguras sobre uma rede peer-to-peer baseada na plataforma android. Undergraduate Work, UFMA, Brazil (2013)
6. OHA: Open Handset Alliance (2011). http://www.openhandsetalliance.com/
7. UPnP: Open Connectivity Foundation (2017). https://openconnectivity.org/
8. Zhang, M., Feng, B.: A P2P VoD system using dynamic priority. In: IEEE 9th Malaysia International Conference on Communications (MICC), pp. 518–523 (2009)

A Proposed Architecture for Robots as a Service

Brunno Vanelli[1], Mariana Rodrigues[2], Madalena Pereira da Silva[1(✉)],
Alex Pinto[1], and M.A.R. Dantas[1]

[1] Federal University of Santa Catarina (UFSC), Blumenau, Brazil
brunno.v@grad.ufsc.br, madalena.silva@posgrad.ufsc.br,
{a.r.pinto,mario.dantas}@ufsc.br
[2] University of Sao Paulo (USP), São Paulo, Brazil
rodrigues.mariana@usp.br

Abstract. This paper presents an architecture for robots as a service
(RaaS) in the cloud, implemented over the MQTT, an open and lightweight protocol for message exchange based on publish/subscribe methods. The system is composed by the cloud layer, hosting the MQTT
Broker, Gateway layer, composed by the IoT gateway to interface Zigbee to Internet, and a local layer, composed by the robots communicating
through a Zigbee network. In order to evaluate the proposed system, metrics regarding the MQTT reliability and quality of service were collected
and analyzed. Finally, a robot prototype was developed and controlled
to test the case-scenario.

Keywords: IoT · MQTT · RaaS · Zigbee

1 Introduction

We have witnessed major developments in computational technologies in the
past years. Specifically, advances in processing, storing and networking technologies made small devices more powerful, enabling a new set of applications
and research fields. One example is the Internet of Things (IoT), a network
interconnecting uniquely identifiable devices or things, which can be "smart"
(capable of sensing/actuating, processing and communicating) or not, in order
to share information or perform tasks in order to achieve a common goal [1,4].
IoT is believed to be a key contributor in many areas, improving the quality of
life and aiding the world's economy [1].

Besides its potential contributions, IoT also has brings many challenges.
When considering the technology acceptance from the general public, security
and trust as well as the lack of standardization are the main obstacles. The
lack of a standardized architecture also affects the management and the interoperability of heterogeneous objects. Quality of Service (QoS) to assure device's
availability and reliability is even more challenging when considering the possible
mobility of IoT nodes, whose huge number will impact and demand adaptations

© Springer International Publishing AG 2017
K. Branco et al. (Eds.): WoCCES 2013-2016, CCIS 702, pp. 117–130, 2017.
DOI: 10.1007/978-3-319-61403-8_7

in today's Internet architecture, such as the use of IPv6 for addressing the connected devices [1]. Finally, how to process all acquired data and accessing IoT devices from anywhere is also a pivotal challenge [2].

Cloud Computing (CC) is considered a important element of IoT systems [1] and one of the most prominent ICT technologies [2]. It provides to its users several virtualized resources such as software or infrastructure equipment in a tailored, reliable way at a low cost [1]. When integrated to a CC platform, the usually resource-constrained IoT devices have at their disposal virtually unlimited processing and storage capabilities. Also, heterogeneous IoT devices can be virtualized and made available to the end-user in a homogeneous way even without standard interfaces, being able to attend requests device-independently [2,3].

Robots and robotic systems have had little exposure to the general public, since they are usually built for specific, predetermined applications in controlled environments, are difficult to be operated or configured by lay people and are very costly when more powerful components are needed for more sophisticated tasks [2]. The use of Internet resources in what is called Cloud Robotics (CR) made possible for robots to use the Cloud for resource-demanding tasks, such as high complexity calculations or object recognition [14], simplifying their design and manufacturing [6,9] and making way for their use in social situations and smart environments to be explored.

Even though Cloud Robotics allowed great advances in Robotics, it still has many issues such as interoperability between heterogeneous devices, QoS and standardization. As with IoT devices, robots virtualization can solve interoperability issues and provide users with different robots or robotic systems in a friendly homogeneous way through services, in the concept of Robot as a Service (RaaS) [3,5] though the IoT infrastructure.

In this paper, a RaaS implementation over Message Queue Telemetry Transport (MQTT) protocol is presented. In order to evaluate the proposed architecture, we developed a case-scenario where the service consumer may connect to the cloud service and control the vehicle remotely to sweep an area, as well as request sensor data (humidity and temperature) from the ambient.

This paper is organized as follows. Section 2 presents an overview of the MQTT protocol, such as publish/subscribe methods, as well as message exchange and Quality of service parameters. Section 3 shows the proposed architecture and a breakdown of its layers and components. Section 4 presents an analysis of the MQTT protocol for the proposed scenario. Section 5 presents a real-world application prototype to validate the proposal. Finally, Sect. 6 presents the conclusions and future work.

2   Background Information

2.1   Publish/Subscribe Systems

Publish/Subscribe (pub/sub) systems are constituted by three components: *publishers* which share relevant information, *subscribers* which consume the information, and a *broker* that mediates the information exchange [8]. Subscribers register their interest in a event by invoking `subscribe()` operation and publishers share their events by invoking `publish()` operation—the same node can act as a publisher and a subscriber at distinct moments [8]. When an event is published, the broker propagates it to all subscribers.

Pub/sub architectures implement three types of decoupling: *space decoupling* (nodes generating and consuming events are not aware of each other, even if they are in the same device), *time decoupling* (nodes do not necessarily need to be active at the same time to share data) and *synchronization decoupling* (no nodes are blocked or put on hold due to the event delivery system). With those dependencies between nodes eliminated, the system becomes more scalable and well adapted to distributed environments with asynchronous communication or intermittent nodes [7]. There are three types of subscribing schemes in pub/sub systems [7]:

- *topic-based:* event distribution is based on *topics*, which are identified by keywords reflecting a hierarchical structure; it enforces interoperability because of string keywords, but have a static scheme (the nodes have to know which topics to publish or subscribe in advance) that limits its expressiveness.
- *content-based:* event distribution is based on *content*, which can be internal attributes or metadata, for example; event selection is specified by a subscription language that allows the combination of properties into subscription patters; however, it has a higher runtime overhead due to its complexity.
- *type-based:* event distribution is based on its *type* (like temperature data, for example); when subscribing to a type T, nodes express interest in all instances of any types that conform to T.

2.2   Message Queue Telemetry Transport (MQTT) Protocol

The Message Queue Telemetry Transport (MQTT) Protocol is a lightweight topic-based publish/subscribe protocol that provides many-to-many communication [1, 10, 11] whose main purpose is telemetry or remote monitoring. The protocol was designed for resource-constrained devices by providing a reliable data stream over TCP with compact packet payload and a simple API. MQTT-based brokers can support many thousand of concurrent device connections, making them suitable for large networks of small devices, such as in the IoT [13].

Quality of Service. MQTT implements three different types of QoS [12]:

- *'At most once' (level 0):* this is the simplest QoS level. The receiver does not acknowledge any message, and the sender does not perform any retry. The messages are delivered either once or not at all to their destination.
- *'At least once' (level 1):* in this QoS, the message is retransmitted until the receiver acknowledges it. The messages are guaranteed to be delivered, but there can be duplicates.
- *'Exactly once' (level 2):* in this QoS, there is an acknowledgment for message reception and completion. The message are guaranteed to be delivered only once. However, this QoS generates an increased overhead.

The application selects the appropriate QoS for its publications and subscriptions. A subscriber specifies the desired QoS when subscribing topic, as does a publisher when sharing a message. When sending messages to multiple recipients, the broker treats each one and their desired QoS level differently [12].

Message Exchange. MQTT relies on a small set of messages to manage device connection and the publish/subscriber scheme [12]. Figure 1 illustrates the message exchange between publisher and subscribers. In order to illustrate the different QoS levels, three subscribers are inserted. Sub_0 has QoS level 0 (At most once), Sub_1 has QoS level 1 (At least once) and Sub_2 has QoS level 2 (Exactly once).

Client Connection. cfrom clients (publishers or subscribers) to the server is a CONNECT Package (messages 1–4 in Fig. 1). This package can be sent only once over a network connection, otherwise configuring a protocol violation. This message contain a number of parameters that specify the connection behaviour, such as the presence of a username and password, Last Will and Testament configuration (a message to be sent when the client do not disconnect cleanly), and the Keep Alive interval (time interval that represents the maximum time between client packages). The server in turn send the CONNACK Package (messages 1.1–4.1 in Fig. 1) stating if the connection was accepted or the reason it was refused. If no CONNAC Package is received, the client should close the network connection.

Topic Subscription. In order to subscribe to one or more topics, subscribers must send a SUBSCRIBE Package (messages 5–7 in Fig. 1), specifying a maximum QoS for each topic of interest. At least one topic/QoS pair must be present in SUBSCRIBE Packet. Server sends a SUBACK Package (messages 5.1–7.1 in Fig. 1) to subscribers after receiving and processing a SUBSCRIBE Packet. If the subscription was accepted, the last topic contained message (if any) is sent to the new subscriber.

Topic Publishing. In order to publish an application message to a topic, publishers must send a PUBLISH Package (message 9 in Fig. 1), specifying if the message is to be retained in the topic, if the package is a retry and the desired QoS. Broker response for PUBLISH Package will depend on QoS level of both server (publish/subscribers and nodes).

QoS = 0—No acknowledgment packages are sent.
QoS = 1—PUBACK package is sent as an acknowledgment that the message was delivered.
QoS = 2—In order to ensure the message is delivered exactly once, sender and receiver exchange three more packets: PUBREC (Publish received), PUBREL (Publish release) and PUBCOMP (Publish complete).

When considering a sender/receiver pair, the one with the lowest QoS will determine which messages will be exchanged (if any) after a PUBLISH Package. The broker is considered to have a QoS 2 when receiving and equals to the message when delivering a PUBLISH Package. Figure 1 clearly explicits the packages

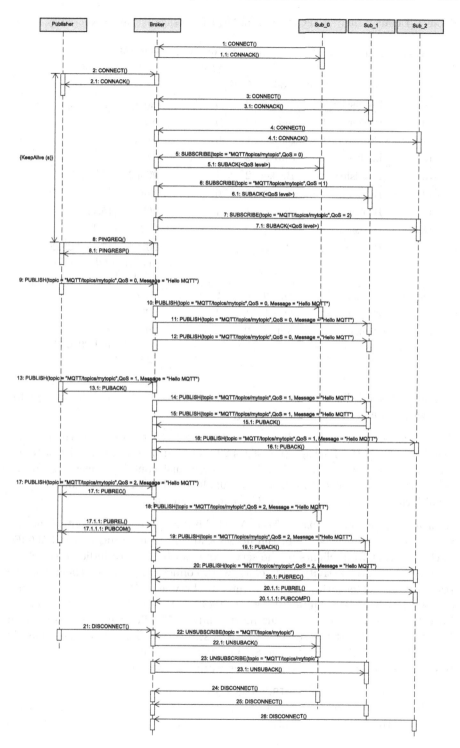

Fig. 1. Message exchange in MQTT protocol.

Table 1. Detailed analysis of QoS levels in MQTT message exchange exposed by Fig. 1.

Message	Sender		Receiver		Resulting QoS	PUBLISH acknowledgement
	Node	QoS	Node	QoS		
9	Publisher	0	Broker	2	0	None
10	Broker	0	Sub_0	0	0	None
11	Broker	0	Sub_1	1	0	None
12	Broker	0	Sub_2	2	0	None
13	Publisher	1	Broker	2	1	PUBACK (13.1)
14	Broker	1	Sub_0	0	0	None
15	Broker	1	Sub_1	1	1	PUBACK (15.1)
16	Broker	1	Sub_2	2	1	PUBACK (16.1)
17	Publisher	2	Broker	2	2	PUBREC (17.1), PUBREL (17.1.1) and PUBCOM (17.1.1.1)
18	Broker	2	Sub_0	0	0	None
19	Broker	2	Sub_1	1	1	PUBACK (19.1)
20	Broker	2	Sub_2	2	2	PUBREC (20.1), PUBREL (20.1.1) and PUBCOM (20.1.1.1)

exchanged for all different QoS combinations. Table 1 details QoS analisys for messages exchanged in topic publishing.

Topic Unsubscription. In order to unsubscribe from topics, subscribers must send a UNSUBSCRIBE Package (messages 22 and 23 in Fig. 1) with a list of topics they are no longer interested in. The message must contain at least one topic. Server will answer this request with an UNSUBACK Package to acknowledge the unsubscription request (messages 22.1 and 23.1 in Fig. 1).

Network Connection Activity Check. MQTT has a special 'ping' control mechanism to determine the state of the network and its composing nodes. PINGREQ Package is sent from clients to the server and can be used to indicate (a) client activity, (b) server activity and (c) network connectivity. Every client has the responsibility of ensuring that the interval between Control Packets do not exceed the Keep Alive interval set in CONNECT Package. If no other Control Packets are being sent, the client must send a PINGREQ Packet (message 8 in Fig. 1) in order to let the server know it is still active. The server must answer with a PINGRESP Packet (message 8.1 in Fig. 1), which can be used by the client to diagnose the server status and the network connectivity.

Disconnection. Clients send DISCONNECT Packet (messages 21, 24–26 in Fig. 1) to indicate to the server a clean disconnection. After sending this packet, clients must close the network connection and can't send any more Control Packets to the server.

3   Proposed Architecture

In order to propose an implementation for robots as service in the cloud, there are a few requirements to satisfy: reliability, security, availability and latency compatible with the application.

The MQTT protocol standard already satisfy some of the requirements needed, implementing QoS to guarantee reliability, natively supporting TLS/SSL over TCP, that guarantees safety in the communication and authenticity of the broker. Moreover, MQTT also provides authentication in the connection with the broker allowing for a user-password pair, that makes it unavailable to unauthenticated users.

The architecture is implemented as shown in Fig. 2. Specific topics are used for specific applications, meaning a privilege system can be implemented: topics can be limited to read-only for some users, read and write for the client and the robot, and write-only for other sensors over the network.

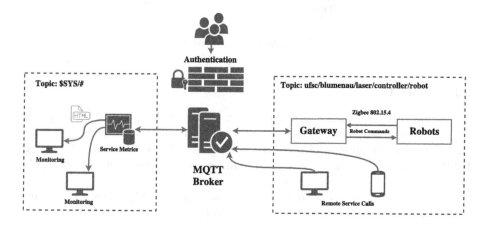

Fig. 2. Proposed architecture.

The architecture proposed has a few advantages and disadvantages. One of the advantages is that it can deal with the dynamic nature of IP acquisition for connected nodes, providing full-duplex communication even for devices behind NATs. This means that MQTT is also more suitable than HTTP because messages are delivered as soon as they reach the broker, and no pooling is necessary like in HTTP.

One disadvantage is that the latency is drastically increased when using a broker to relay messages instead of direct communication, since each packet has to travel to the broker, be processed and travel back to the final node. This may also increase packet loss in noisy environments.

The architecture can be divided into three layers: The Cloud layer, responsible for interconnecting the devices and running the MQTT Broker, the Gateway layer, that creates the connection between the broker and the local network, process the requests and wraps the commands given in the Zigbee protocol. Finally, there is the Local layer, composed by a 802.15.4 Zigbee network to control the robots. Figure 3 illustrates the whole layer system. There is also an additional application layer, where Web or Desktop applications can be written to better control and monitor the whole system.

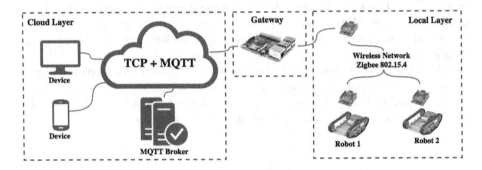

Fig. 3. Architecture layers.

3.1 Cloud Layer

The cloud layer includes the whole server back-end. It is meant to host the MQTT Broker and re-route the messages between nodes quickly and securely. Among the many options of brokers available, we choose Mosquitto for being lightweight and providing efficient communication, with low memory and CPU use. It also supports TLS encryption natively.

In this experiment, we used a virtual machine provided by Microsoft's Azure team. The system is composed by a Standard DS1 v2 (1 core, 3.5 GB memory) machine, running Ubuntu 14.04.

3.2 Gateway Layer

This layer is responsible for interconnecting both the cloud layer and local layer. It is composed by a Raspberry Pi B+, connected to the internet via ethernet cable. This layer is needed to protect the local layer, normally composed by constrained devices both in memory, CPU and power, from incoming traffic and possible overloads, or even malicious connections. And since the local layer is constrained and has limitations, it can take several milliseconds to process a large task, increasing the latency considerably.

However, the most important task of the gateway is translate protocols between the TCP/IP stream and Zigbee protocol, and it also includes processing and translating the commands received to contain less information, considering the low-rate transmission Zigbee offers. In order to connect the device to the

MQTT broker, we used a Python script making use of Python library Paho MQTT, also available in many other languages like C++, Javascript and Java.

In order to serialize the commands in the MQTT messages we used JSON encoding, since it provides readable information format, fast decode times and useful key-pair schema. Figure 4 illustrates the whole translation process.

Notice that there is a response by the Robot when the `collectData` flag is enabled. This is telling the robot to collect data from its sensors and send the information back to the client that requested it, answering with a Zigbee packet to the gateway, translated to another JSON object and sent over to the broker, to finally get back to the client.

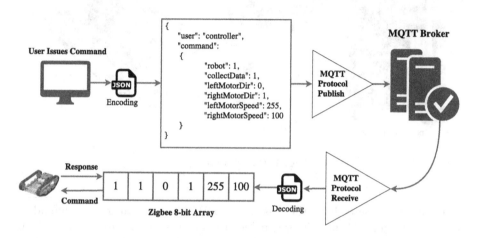

Fig. 4. Communication order.

The gateway is threaded and event driven. It respond to the following events:

- *On Connect:* subscribe to the robot topic when connecting to the broker.
- *On Message Received:* decode and parse the message received from the remote controller, sending the command over Zigbee if matching the correct requirements.
- *On Message Received (Zigbee):* parse and encode response from the wireless Zigbee network, sending back to the broker to be routed to connected controller.

3.3 Local Layer

The local layer is composed by a wireless network composed by 802.15.4 XBee 1mW Series 1 Modules, controlled by Arduinos Leonardo through the XBee library. Zigbee was chosen for the local layer because its modules are low-power, ideal for devices limited on energy.

In order to connect the Arduinos to the XBee module, we used a Sparkfun XBee Shield. For the robots, we used an additional Sparkfun Motor Shield to control the robot motors. The robot base is composed by a Tamya Motor set, that provides tracks, wheels and a base. Figure 5 shows the parts breakdown and the finished robot.

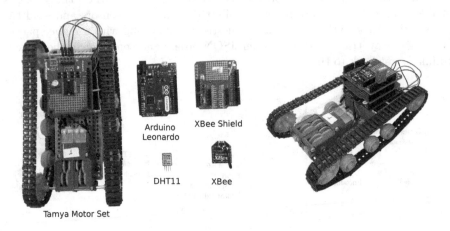

Arduino Leonardo

XBee Shield

DHT11

XBee

Tamya Motor Set

Fig. 5. Robot prototype.

In order to sense data, there is also a DHT11 temperature and humidity sensor. It has a NTC thermistor capable of reading temperature ranging from 0 to 50 °C, ±2 °C, and a humidity HR20 sensor, capable of reading values between 20 and 90%, ±5%. It also has an internal circuit to serialize and send this data to the Arduino, where it can be read with the DHT library.

Even though Arduino doesn't support threads, there are two virtual events programmed:

– *On Message Received:* parse received message and drive the motors accordingly.
– *On collectData Flag:* collect sensor data and send response message.

4 MQTT Performance Analysis

In order to evaluate the proposed system, there are three basic metrics to consider: latency, packet loss and jitter. Figure 6 shows how latency increases as QoS increases. From the three, QoS = 0 shows the lowest latency and lowest jitter, since less confirmations are needed in order to deliver the messages. For QoS = 1 and QoS = 2, the travel time is much higher because the broker has to guarantee all clients received the message, making it not suitable for critical real-time applications.

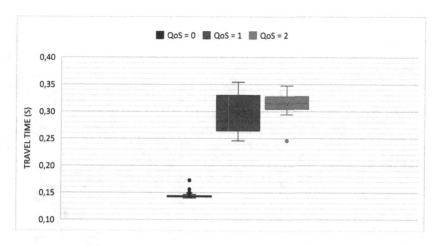

Fig. 6. Travel time for different QoS values.

The packet loss had little impact over the experiments. Even for QoS = 0, where messages are not guaranteed to be delivered to every client, there was no packet loss even for message bursts, where one message was being sent every millisecond. This reflects the reliability of the TCP/IP protocol when delivering messages, as well as the great capacity of the MQTT broker to deal with incoming messages. That said, QoS = 1 provides the best option in this scenario, since there is no need for message queuing and the gateway has a wired connection, reducing packet loss probability.

It's important to notice that, even though the QoS = 0 results in this experiment are very consistent, real-time applications could suffer because this approach is not deterministic, and network lags could drastically increase the travel time, if not break the communication link, thus reducing the quality of service. One possible solution to this problem is hosting the MQTT broker locally, in a controlled ambient, making it more reliable for critical applications.

5   Case-Scenario Test

In order to test the robot in the case-scenario, it had to perform a previously selected path and perform sensor reading whenever requested throughout the test. The path chosen can be seen on Fig. 7. The robot could successfully navigate the path and collect the data whenever requested. The results of the sensor measurements can be seen on Fig. 8.

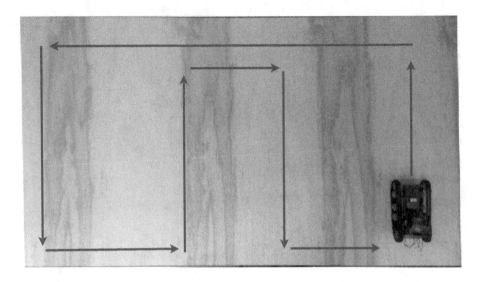

Fig. 7. Robot path.

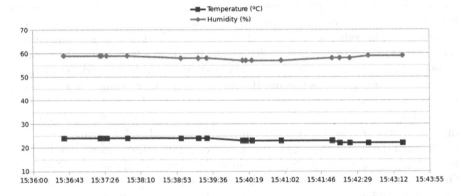

Fig. 8. Temperature and humidity sensing following the path.

6   Conclusions and Future Work

This paper presented an infrastructure to remotely control a robot and retrieve sensor data combining the MQTT protocol over the Internet and Zigbee 802.15.4 locally.

In order to propose an implementation for Robots as service in the cloud, there are a few requirements to satisfy, such as reliability, security, availability and latency compatible with the application. We adopted MQTT because it already defines QoS parameters, supports encryption and authentication natively and has low code footprint and low network bandwidth usage, ideal for constrained devices.

Metrics related to quality of transmission were collected and analysed in order to validate the MQTT broker in the proposed scenario. Finally, the tests in the robot prototype shown that the system is appropriate under the specified conditions.

As for future work, we pretend to add more diverse nodes to the system, as well as add a more functionality, sensing and intelligence to the robots.

Acknowledgements. We would like to thanks to Microsoft Research for Azure Award, providing the virtual machines and data storage used in this experiments.

References

1. Al-Fuqaha, A., Guizani, M., Mohammadi, M., Aledhari, M., Ayyash, M.: Internet of things: a survey on enabling technologies, protocols, and applications. IEEE Commun. Surv. Tutorials **17**(4), 2347–2376 (2015). doi:10.1109/COMST.2015. 2444095. http://dx.doi.org/10.1109/COMST.2015.2444095
2. Chaâri, R., Ellouze, F., Koubâa, A., Qureshi, B., Pereira, N., Youssef, H., Tovar, E.: Cyber-physical systems clouds: a survey. Comput. Netw. **108**, 260–278 (2016). doi:10.1016/j.comnet.2016.08.017. http://linkinghub.elsevier.com/retrieve/pii/S1389128616302699
3. Chen, Y., Du, Z., García-Acosta, M.: Robot as a service in cloud computing. In: Proceedings - 5th IEEE International Symposium on Service-Oriented System Engineering, SOSE 2010, pp. 151–158 (2010). doi:10.1109/SOSE.2010.44
4. Chen, Y., Hu, H.: Internet of intelligent things and robot as a service. Simul. Modell. Pract. Theory **34**, 159–171 (2012). doi:10.1016/j.simpat.2012.03.006. http://dx.doi.org/10.1016/j.simpat.2012.03.006
5. Doriya, R., Chakraborty, P., Nandi, G.C.: Robotic services in cloud computing paradigm. In: Proceedings - 2012 International Symposium on Cloud and Services Computing, ISCOS 2012, pp. 80–83 (2013). doi:10.1109/ISCOS.2012.24
6. Dyumin, A., Puzikov, L., Rovnyagin, M., Urvanov, G., Chugunkov, I.: Cloud computing architectures for mobile robotics. In: 2015 IEEE NW Russia Young Researchers in Electrical and Electronic Engineering Conference (EIConRusNW), pp. 65–70. IEEE (2015). doi:10.1109/EIConRusNW.2015.7102233. http://www.scopus.com/inward/record.url?eid=2-s2.0-84933574830&partnerID=tZOtx3y1, http://ieeexplore.ieee.org/document/7102233/
7. Eugster, P.T., Felber, P.A., Guerraoui, R., Kermarrec, A.M.: The many faces of publish/subscribe. ACM Comput. Surv. **35**(2), 114–131 (2003). doi:10.1145/857076.857078. http://portal.acm.org/citation.cfm?doid=857076.857078
8. Hunkeler, U., Truong, H.L., Stanford-Clark, A.: MQTT-S—a publish/subscribe protocol for Wireless Sensor Networks. In: 2008 3rd International Conference on Communication Systems Software and Middleware and Workshops (COMSWARE 2008), pp. 791–798 (2008). doi:10.1109/COMSWA.2008.4554519. http://ieeexplore.ieee.org/lpdocs/epic03/wrapper.htm?arnumber=4554519
9. Lorencik, D., Sincak, P.: Cloud robotics: current trends and possible use as a service. In: SAMI 2013 - IEEE 11th International Symposium on Applied Machine Intelligence and Informatics, Proceedings, pp. 85–88 (2013). doi:10.1109/SAMI.2013.6480950
10. Mahmood, Z. (ed.): Connectivity Frameworks for Smart Devices. CCN. Springer, Cham (2016). doi:10.1007/978-3-319-33124-9

11. Manzoor, A.: Securing device connectivity in the industrial internet of things (IoT). In: Mahmood, Z. (ed.) Connectivity Frameworks for Smart Devices. CCN, pp. 3–22. Springer, Cham (2016). doi:10.1007/978-3-319-33124-9_1
12. OASIS: MQTT Version 3.1.1 (2014). http://docs.oasis-open.org/mqtt/mqtt/v3.1.1/os/mqtt-v3.1.1-os.html
13. Rajaraajeswari, S., Selvarani, R., Raj, P.: Integration approaches for the internet of things (IoT) era. In: Mahmood, Z. (ed.) Connectivity Frameworks for Smart Devices. CCN, pp. 117–146. Springer, Cham (2016). doi:10.1007/978-3-319-33124-9_6
14. Wan, J., Tang, S., Yan, H., Li, D., Wang, S., Vasilakos, A.V.: Cloud robotics: current status and open issues. IEEE Access **4**, 2797–2807 (2016). doi:10.1109/ACCESS.2016.2574979

Author Index

Printed in the United States
By Bookmasters